Photo by Marc A. Hefty

A pioneer figure in the study of the soul, **Robert Sardello** is a cofounder of the School for Spiritual Psychology, which has programs worldwide. He is a frequent lecturer at the Chalice of Repose Project, in Montana, and at the Dallas Institute of Humanities and Culture. The author of two previous books, *Facing the World with Soul* and *Love and the Soul*, he lives in Greensboro, North Carolina.

FREEING THE SOUL FROM FEAR

Robert Sardello

RIVERHEAD BOOKS

New York

RIVERHEAD BOOKS
Published by The Berkley Publishing Group
A division of Penguin Putnam Inc.
375 Hudson Street
New York, New York 10014

First Riverhead hardcover edition: October 1999
First Riverhead trade paperback edition: January 2001
Riverhead trade paperback ISBN: 1-57322-833-8

The Penguin Putnam Inc. World Wide Web site address is
http://www.penguinputnam.com

The Library of Congress has catalogued the
Riverhead hardcover edition as follows:

Sardello, Robert J.
Freeing the soul from fear / Robert Sardello.
p.   cm.
Includes bibliographical references.
ISBN 1-57322-133-3
1. Fear.   I. Title.
BF575.F2S27   1999   99-28404 CIP
152.4'6—dc21

Printed in the United States of America

10   9   8   7   6   5   4

Contents

Introduction

This is a book about love. Although the title says it's about fear, love is the purpose of this book. For fear can teach us to love in entirely new ways, and that, I think, is the ultimate secret of fear. When we don't run from fear, or try to eradicate it, we discover ourselves anew. We discover ourselves as beings of love.

Before this discovery, however, a crucial intermediate step must be taken, and the place where this step occurs is the imagination. While fear makes the imagination go wild at first, the longer we live under a constant threat—whether it's physical, emotional, or psychological—the more the imagination shuts down. This contraction of the imagination is also a contraction of the life of the soul, and under such conditions we can never get to a place of loving. We have to work a great deal with the life of the soul and the imagination before we can find the depths of love or learn how to enact it toward others and the larger world. Why? Because above all, love is an act of the soul—an experience through which another person, or a spiritual being, or God, lives within us.

The most central spiritual task of our time is working with fear. This work has to be approached in a certain way, of course. If we try to insulate ourselves from fear, the strengths we need to remain fully human—vitality of body, a deep and rich inner self, and an openness to the spiritual dimensions of life—will wither and die. We will become ever further separated from each other, distrustful, concerned about security of every sort—and finally, unable, really, to love.

The forces in the modern world that cause fear are often so large that we feel powerless to stop them. Most of us can have little effect on the hole in the ozone layer, the strife in Israel, the war in Kosovo, anonymous acts of terrorism, corporate downsizing, crazy stock markets, threats of worldwide computer glitches, earthquakes, hurricanes, tornadoes and changing weather patterns, road rage, new viruses, mass murderers, and all the rest.

Whether these events affect us directly or do not seem to involve us at all, the soul is greatly affected. Such is its subtlety and sensitivity. If we are touched in any way, even just through hearing about it, speaking with others, watching the news on television, or reading a newspaper or magazine—the fearful qualities of the event live on in soul life. The fear may not even necessarily live on as a conscious memory. The effect of these events is more a contraction, a shutting down of emotional depth in our lives. Gradually, and imperceptibly, our lives begin to feel flat. As we go about doing the same things we have always done, our feelings diminish, and even if we're in the midst of a great deal of activity, we experience a kind of isolation. We don't know what is happening to us, or why. A mild depression sets in, and if we look inward at all we discover a great deal of fear. More likely, however, we do not bother to look inward. On the surface, everything seems all right. The suffering of the soul goes unnoticed.

People whose souls are extremely sensitive to fear sometimes develop the illness obsessive-compulsive disorder. The medical and psychological world is baffled about the cause of this syndrome. There is some speculation that it is related to the streptococcus bacteria which, if it infects a person in early childhood, might have an effect on a portion of the brain concerned with responding to fear. Whether or not this speculation proves true, it doesn't begin to explain the extent to which obsessive-compulsive disorder can overtake the soul. Those with the illness are completely afraid of the world. Individuals with this malady might, for example, refuse to leave their homes for months on end. They may also develop elaborate rituals to prevent being invaded by whatever fear torments them—touching a doorknob, breathing the air, eating food, just about anything. These people, it is clear, fear fear itself. They may say they are deathly afraid of germs or a virus but that is merely a way of saying the cause of their terror is something invisible. If we were to look at such people more as cultural guides, rather than as individuals with strange and peculiar psychological symptoms, however, we might learn a lot.

In this book, I look at all types of fear—not just those suffered by victims of obsessive-compulsive disorder. Rather than looking at people, things, and events around us that pose a threat to our well-being as the causes of fear, I instead look at them as the bearers of fear—the messenger instead of the message. What we usually think of as fear is merely our response to the presence of fear, which exists in the world autonomously from us.

This manner of looking at fear—that it is not just our response to something that threatens our well-being but also something quite real in its own right—is an unusual way of considering this phenomenon. We are accustomed to thinking in terms of causes and effects. In the case of fear, we have the rather simplistic notion that if the causes of fear can be found and eliminated, fear would thus be eliminated. What must be remembered while reading this book is that I am speaking of fear always at the level of the soul. The soul does not follow the logic of cause and effect as we think of it in the physical world.

The treatment of people with obsessive-compulsive disorder is instructive in understanding the peculiar power that fear can have over us. The conventional treatment for this syndrome is conditioning. If, for example, a person fears touching a doorknob, not because of what might be on the other side of the door but because of some invisible contaminant on the knob, therapy consists of encouraging the sufferer to gradually come closer and closer to the door, touch the doorknob, and finally open the door. This treatment may take months. Further, a person with this illness usually feels the same trepidation toward many things. A person with obsessive-compulsive disorder, might well, for example, have a ten-page list of all the things that are feared, and usually each of these fears must be treated individually. The logic of this course of therapy is that if a physical object is the cause of the fear, targeting the object through conditioning attacks the problem at its source. In this kind of linear thinking, however, it becomes necessary to treat every object associated with a fear.

From the viewpoint of the soul, something different transpires. Fear contracts the soul. This contraction expresses itself as an inability to engage with others and with the world. One's world becomes increasingly diminished. The encouragement of the therapist to come out into the world again is an act of love that makes possible an imagination of the real. The role of the therapist is to reawaken the patient's sense of how he imagines the real and to allow him to accept his own fear; a doorknob is first and foremost a thing used to open doors and not the harbinger of deadly viruses. This re-imagining is really a way of putting fear back into its proper place. Yes, there may be germs on the doorknob, and it's *possible* that we'll die if we touch it. The point is, fear is always present in the world, and having the courage to meet the world is an inescapable part of life. The caring and loving relationship between the therapist and the suffering person allows an expansion of the soul and a restoration of the imagination, which results in a healthy relation with the wider world.

In this book, I do not focus directly on the treatment of obsessive-compulsive disorder or on any of the familiar psychological ways of analyzing fear—such as anxiety, phobias, or traumatic stress syndrome. My premise is that fear is increasing in the world, and at a very rapid rate. Besides showing up as individual psychological difficulties, we now have to contend with this destructive force as a cultural phenomenon that touches us all, more deeply and significantly than we might ever imagine. The soul life of humanity is in jeopardy.

Popular writing on the subject of the soul, which is also increasing, stands as a testament to our collective plight. People are encouraged to do soul work with the understanding that unless we take up responsibility for soul life, it will disintegrate. At the same time, most of the writing in this genre says very little about *how* to go about strengthening the life of the soul. And none of it focuses on fear as a terrible obstacle to experiencing and caring for the soul.

Our current attitude toward the soul is that it's a permanent element of the human being. We can lose our connection with soul, the thinking goes, but there are ways to return to this connection, such as honoring our suffering, being open to the enchantment of the world, viewing our quirkiness as character rather than deficiency, paying attention to dream life, taking up some artistic activity, valuing the imagination.

As important as such endeavors may be, simply turning toward soul is not always effective in the presence of so many strong fears. Therefore, I depart from this way of thinking and make specific recommendations of how to go about attending to soul life and strengthening its force. In the chapters that follow, you will find a consistent method for countering the presence of fears, which can be summed up as follows.

First, we must work to become aware of the particular manner in which different kinds of fear affect the soul. With each kind of fear, a natural capacity of the soul becomes weakened. Second, we must find ways to reinstate the diminished soul capacity through conscious activity. In each instance, the idea is to engage in an imaginative exercise that reawakens the soul quality that has become numb. Third, in addition to simply doing the exercises, it is necessary to reflect on our soul life and to describe for ourselves what happens in us.

The immediate outcome of the exercises is not so important. In fact, nothing spectacular happens while doing them. The effects occur gradually, over a period of time. But, when we become familiar with how inner life alters through the exercises, we can begin to discover how the awakened soul capacity can be engaged in our daily lives. As soul capacities awaken, so does our ability to become more loving and to bring forth love as an effective antidote to the spread of fear.

One question you may have as you work with this book is whether it is necessary to do all the suggested exercises. The answer is that you may do better if you simply take one of them—whichever one makes most sense at this moment in your life—and work with it for a while. It need not take very long. We are accustomed to thinking of meditation periods as lasting a half hour or more. But the soul responds better if an exercise is done on a regular basis, daily if possible, but for no more than about five minutes. Such brief sessions might seem paltry. Remember, however, that soul time is quite different from clock time. These exercises are not like going to the gym for a workout. Their benefits don't increase if we repeat them to exhaustion.

The imaginative exercises in this book have been practiced by individuals all over the country, in seminars sponsored by the School of Spiritual Psychology, an organization run by Cheryl Sanders and me. In all, over three hundred people have done the exercises. These people come from every walk of life. None of them has been diagnosed with specific phobias, but all express deep concern over the way in which fears enter their daily lives. People attend the seminars offered by the school out of an interest in developing soul consciousness and spiritual capacities applicable to practical life. The experiences of the participants in these seminars form a part of this book. The approach to the exercises developed for the seminars has a long tradition, many of them having been adapted from the spiritual science of Rudolf Steiner, a gifted Austrian clairvoyant who worked at the same time as Freud and Jung. Engaging with images in the way described is perfectly safe. One remains completely conscious while doing them; no altered state or out-of-body experiences occur. In fact, the whole approach of spiritual psychology is based on developing a conscious, living soul experience that is receptive to spiritual realms. It is important, in working with fear, to do so fully consciously.

One of the great challenges in writing about fear is to avoid generating more fear by doing so. For example, I received a letter from a friend who had just returned from a conference on the so-called Y2K problem. The conference was held at a large church, and speakers from all over the country attended. My friend said the people were warned to stockpile supplies, just to be prepared. The speakers said that they were there just to convey information, so that people could make choices for themselves. The leader of the church then stood up and said that it is also important to recognize the limitations of a strictly materialistic approach to the computer problem, that it is important to have a mystical perspective. God is bigger than Y2K, and He surely is not impotent in this matter. God, the pastor said, is in the computer. My friend came away from the day feeling a great deal of fear. His fear came not from a greater understanding of the possible ramifications of the computer problem, but because, he said, he could sense all the fear working just beneath the surface of their discussion. Fear itself was never addressed, and neither was love. People were given technical information and then told God would provide a solution.

The alternative to hiding from fear, or hoping God will fix it, is to stay open and centered in the body, to be committed to the beauty of the world, and to realize that while fear cannot be completely eliminated, we can work to avoid being overwhelmed by it. To work in a healthy way with fear, one must live in close, conscious connection with soul life and develop spirituality that is an ordinary part of daily life.

Earlier, I stated that love is the antidote to fear. Fear, however, can teach us a great deal about love. Fear can sharpen our alertness, and we can utilize this quickening of consciousness to become more perceptive of the varieties of love. In a later chapter, I explore the modes of love, something that I have learned from many encounters with fear. Love is mentioned in the earlier chapters, but I hold off from taking it up as a main theme because love is too easily understood in an egotistical manner. Sentimental notions of love, or simply using the word without an inner understanding of what it means, or lumping all sorts of different kinds of love together, are ineffective as a deterrent to fear. The notion that fear can do no harm if I just love more intensely and continuously is quite egotistical, not to mention naïve. Love is really very little under our control. At best, we can work to make ourselves adequate vessels of love so that it can flow through us and, ultimately, into the wider world.

One of the trickiest aspects of fear is that it can take hold of us without our being aware of it. People who live constantly under the shadow of fear do not cower and shudder at every moment, but they often live as if in a constant dream state. After a while these people forget that their peculiar state of being is not real. This phenomenon is well documented in psychology. People who have experienced significant trauma live for years in a kind of light trance state, unable to get a real foothold in the world. Such people often have trouble establishing intimate relationships, may become addicted to one thing or another, and often have a cruel side that surfaces from time to time.

Larger, culture-wide instances of trauma also exist: the rise of National Socialism under Adolf Hitler is a clear example. His abuses traumatized an entire nation and brought about unbelievable atrocities, all because of his living in the constant presence of fear. The recent research of psychiatrist Robert Jay Lifton allowed me to realize that the numbness induced by fear is something more than a shutting down of bodily sensitivity and soul awareness. Numbing coincides with a replacement of the self, or the soul, with a false self, and this "doubling" takes place without our realizing it has happened. The cultural implications of fear are enormous. Further, this replacement of the most central aspect of our being does not occur only in the presence of overt hostility. It can arise from far more subtle influences. In a later chapter, I address this concern, showing how doubling occurs in our own culture, and I offer the means necessary for countering the consequent loss of soul.

So many books are published with the word *soul* in the title, written from so many different perspectives, that I think it is necessary to make as clear as possible what I mean by the term *soul*, or at least give some context for how I use the word. In the twentieth century, the word acquired meaning beyond the context of religion due to the highly original depth psychology of C. G. Jung. I certainly have been influenced by Jung and even more so by those who have applied his work in individual psychotherapy to cultural concerns, particularly James Hillman and Thomas Moore. I had the great fortune to work closely with Hillman and Moore over a period of five years in the 1980s at the Dallas Institute of Humanities and Culture. Together, we made significant advances in bringing soul out of the therapy room and into the wider world. This important direction was largely due to the impetus and the genius of Gail Thomas, the primary founder of the Dallas Institute. She urged us all to look at the world—at cities, institutions, architecture, media, modern culture—and see it as the archetypal imagination embodied. She made us see that soul work has practical implications for contemporary cultural life.

Jung was wise enough to avoid defining soul, but his characterization of it is really quite simple and elegant: soul, he says, is image. By that he means that the spontaneous inner appearance of images—sometimes conscious, sometimes not—is the mark of the functioning of soul. Further, by image he does not mean pictures observed through the inner eye, or mental images. By image, Jung means the invisible, orienting patterns through which we experience a sense of personality and also a deeper sense of the world. The soul arises from these enduring patterns, the archetypes. Relating our behavior back to archetypal patterns helps us understand the patterns of our own experience. Images, then, are not what we "see"; they are what we "see through." We experience a sense of soul when we feel the sense of these deeper patterns working through our sensing, thinking, feeling, and acting.

Jung was certainly interested in the wider world. He speculated a good deal about soul in contemporary culture, and traveled to experience the active soul life of other peoples. He also gave accounts of phenomena of interest to culture, such as art, mythological stories, and even unidentified flying objects. But he could not quite get to the soul of the world as autonomous from the individual soul. I mention this limitation because, having relied on Jung's conception of the soul, I found it difficult to identify the soul of contemporary culture when I tried to look at fear as something more than a problem of the individual psyche. But fortunately, I found help with the spiritual science of Rudolf Steiner.

Steiner, who is less well known than Jung, worked, as was stated above, at the same time as Jung and was well aware of his contributions. Steiner was a philosopher, scholar, scientist, educator, and the founder of anthroposophy, a modern spiritual science. He inspired a renewal of many cultural activities, including education (the Waldorf Schools), agriculture (Biodynamics), medicine (Anthroposophical Medicine), special education (the Camphill Movement), art, economics, philosophy, and religion. He speaks about the contributions and limits of Jung's approach to the soul in, among other places, *Psychoanalysis and Spiritual Psychology*.[1] His conception of the soul, which I rely on considerably, is presented in *A Psychology of Body, Soul, and Spirit*.[2] Steiner's description of the soul parallels Jung's only up to a point. He speaks of the inner life of the soul as consisting of an ongoing, dramatic tension between love and hate. Neither of these words is to be taken in its usual everyday sense, for here they mean forces of attraction and repulsion. Together, this tension is expressed in the forming of images.

Moreover, everything that goes on in the world around us, our relationships with others, and the collective forces of culture, affects the soul and lives on within it long after the initial impressing event ceases. A discussion of the long-term effects of the events around us on soul life is surprisingly absent from Jung's psychology, and that is why Steiner's contributions are so important.

Contrary to Freud's psychology, which asserts that unconscious memories are the source of our illnesses, Steiner suggests that what lives on in the soul are not only memory contents but an overall expansion (in the case of healthful experiences) or contraction of the soul (in the case of fears). Such changes, he says, influence our approach and understanding of ourselves, others, and the world. The descriptions of fear in this book are closer to this understanding of the life of the soul. Steiner does not propose a grand theory of the soul, but begins with the question of what can be known of soul life through observation alone, and proceeds from there to give his descriptions. My approach to fear is to *do* as Steiner does—to make close observations, and not simply to adopt his conclusions.

In what follows, you will learn something about the ways of fear, how to work with the imagination, how to move toward an encompassing love of the world, and the necessity of developing beauty with a bite; by this, I mean the necessity of making our lives beautiful as an expression of love in the world. All of these suggestions are simply ways of saying that it takes time to make soul, to live soul, and to experience soul. The fears that predominate today take time away from soulwork. The most severe contraction of soul life has come about very recently, since World War II, although it has been squeezed for centuries. Just think of all that has occurred in the brief span of time since the war. Some of the areas in which we've seen drastic changes: space travel, computers, medical technology, transportation, economic values, genetics, moral values, gender roles, family life, religious values, corporate structures, globalization. Fear arises in the soul when change occurs more rapidly than our soul capacities can keep up with. Many fears we experience now have to do with the future arriving ahead of itself. We are pushed way beyond ourselves, emotionally and psychically, and tremendous stress results from this fundamental discord. Just recently, I read of the introduction of a line of pharmaceuticals for animals: "Doggy-Prozac." The premise for this treatment is that our pets have internalized the stress of modern life and have all sorts of symptoms to show for it: crying, biting, scratching at the door, even injuring themselves. Well, this is our stress, our fear. Perhaps we would do well to look at our animals for a picture of the state of our soul life.

For each of us, it took a tremendous effort as a child to learn to read, to do mathematics, and to think. None of these capacities developed naturally. Learning the ways of the soul in a conscious manner is an adult task, but the effort involved is analogous to the effort involved in our childhood learning. It takes hard work to develop a sense of the soul. If we have an interest in soul at all, there is a tendency to want to bask in hearing about it, which can set up a resonance within our own soul and deceive us into feeling we have had a soul experience. Fear can, just perhaps, be the impetus that shows us that we have to earn the wings of imagination.

CHAPTER 1

Stepping Into the
Perils of Fear

Fear is our dark companion, accompanying us from the moment of waking to the depths of dreaming at night. Here is a small sample of the most common fears: losing one's job; having a child die; growing old; being physically attacked; getting cancer; losing a relationship; not being good enough; not being able to take care of one's family. The list goes on and on. Being free from fear might at first seem to mean getting rid of this dark companion once and for all. We thus spend our time seeking more and more comfort. We seek distraction in shopping, entertainment, or vacations. We purchase expensive automobiles, eat out frequently, spend too much time watching television, move out to a gated housing development where it is "safe." We go into therapy or join a support group, take

Prozac, carry a gun, live in denial and isolation. But such measures only momentarily dull the presence of fear, allowing it to grow more intense underneath, and furthering the need for more comfort.

Since the world is filled with situations that will inevitably arouse fear, there can be no escape. Thus, becoming free of fear cannot mean abolishing fear. That would be equivalent to saying that the only way to feel free in a marriage is to dissolve the marriage. We can, however, develop inner resources to help us face fear. How to go about doing so forms the focus of this book.

The Gospels are quite correct in asserting that "*perfect love casts out fear.*" But since few of us are capable of attaining perfect love, the abolition of fear seems unattainable. Yet if it is not faced, fear feeds on itself, gnaws away at the very substance of our being, and can completely overwhelm us. Over time, fear can rob us of our humanity. However, when we approach it with the resources of a more conscious soul life, fear no longer takes us over but instead challenges us to continually discover more of our humanity.

Fear stirs up many reactions that can drain and confuse the soul. In order to develop a truly deep consciousness, we need to embrace a more comprehensive picture of the soul in human life. The soul is usually equated with qualities of inner experience—with the imagination, with feelings that carry a reflective component, and with what lies beyond conscious experience. In this sense, the soul shapes the way we approach and respond to outer events. I take a somewhat broad view of the soul, including within it influences coming to us from the outer world. Such events in the world continue to live on in the soul, and not just as memories, but as contractions or expansions of the field of the soul. Fear contracts the soul. When we're afraid, we experience ourselves as more alone, more isolated, less engaged with the wider world, and more cut off from the riches of our inner lives. When the soul expands, however, it offers us a way to work with the destructive forces within each of us. The soul thrives on qualities such as joy, compassion, truth, pleasure, giving, serving, beauty, and even inner struggle. Most of all, the soul finds expression in a wide range of acts of love— making deep connections with others, developing capacities to serve, opening our heart to the spiritual realms. Learning to consciously hold on to and develop these qualities in new ways can go a long way toward healing fear in the world.[1]

We begin with the simple definition of fear as that which dulls the immediate experience of our true human identity—of who we are as individuals. To be fully human requires a sense of the mystery of our body in relation to the grandeur of the world and of the cosmos. Human identity also requires presence to the inner qualities of experience—feeling, emotion, creative thinking, memory, a sense of destiny, and all the subtle qualities that make the difference between experiencing life as a random string of events and experiencing life as significant. Our true humanity also consists of being oriented toward and experiencing the reality of something larger than ourselves—the mystery of otherness, the reality of the sacred, a sense of the holy.

When fear strikes us, our sense of being fully human is assaulted. Here is an example of such an instance of fear, written by one of the people in our workshops. The instance is instructive because it is not particularly unusual and yet contains elements common to all experiences of fear:

It was a later summer day somewhere on a road in Colorado. It was afternoon. My boyfriend and I were on our way back from Denver. A good holiday was over. We were talking about his parents whom we had visited for two days. We had left just two hours before. I was driving. It was getting late in the day when we hit the freeway. My boyfriend was talking. I remember that I was laughing about something. We were on the entrance lane. I accelerated. I looked in the outer mirror—the lane behind us was clear. I turned my head, looked over my shoulder— clear. Setting my signal lights, looking in the back mirror again, I slowly pulled over. I sat upright again and looked forward into the lane in front of us—right onto the bumper of a huge truck. Our car seemed to be touching it already. Everything else vanished. There was no sound, no light, no surroundings anymore. There was only the truck, the clutch, the brake, the steering wheel, the gear shift and I. My heart did not race; rather, it stopped beating at all. I did not sweat; I was icy cold. My hands, my mouth, my eyes were as dry as a desert. My body was not really stiff; it functioned perfectly. But it just did what was necessary, nothing more. For a time which seemed to be endless I was alone with the truck, trying to get away from it. When it was finally about fifteen feet ahead the world seemed to come back to me. With the sounds, the surroundings and the light, time and my consciousness came back as well. Time showed me that I was still going rather fast, around fifty miles per hour. My consciousness told me that we had just escaped certain death. My physical reactions changed. I started trembling, I was freezing cold and sweating at the same time. I had difficulties keeping the car on the road. At the next pullout I stopped the car and just sat there for a few minutes shaking, weeping, being comforted by my boyfriend. The situation had occurred so spontaneously that I did not have a chance to experience fear until it was over. The dangerous situation lasted not more than a minute; but it took me about an hour to go back to a state where my body and spirit were working within limits. [2]

Even in this momentary experience, it is easy to see how fear constricts the soul. Our senses are narrowed, time changes, we are suddenly isolated, the width and breadth of consciousness disappear. Fear races through the body, producing waves of trembling, a momentary breakdown. In this description, the loving presence of a friend helps bring the person back to a normal state, but the effects of the fear continue to reverberate in the body. Imagine what fear does when it is not just a momentary occurrence as it is here, but a continual, underlying presence in life. The same factors operate as they do in this description, though at a more subtle level, producing dire effects on the body, the soul, and the spirit. Like the woman in the car, we become oriented only toward survival. Our body becomes armored. We lose contact with our inner life, and our connection with others and the world diminishes.

As a society, our answer to the presence of many kinds of ongoing fear has been to cover them over rather than to work with them in ways that could restore and enlarge our capacities of soul.

So many things in the world impair our ability to face fear. Our senses, for example, are already constricted from overstimulation and excess. Our culture is so oriented toward influencing masses of people, and moves so quickly and efficiently, that little time or space remains for inner life. Even our most valued cultural institutions, such as education, religion, and politics, obscure our inner development when they are governed by fear. Fear,

I propose, re-makes the sensory, cultural, and sacred realms, diminishing them all.

Every human act alters the world. Everything we do in the course of the day enters into and becomes part of the world. If we act out of fear, fear becomes inscribed into the world. If we act out of love and beauty, that also becomes imprinted. A kind of circular current is established, through which the results of our actions can become apparent to us, and, in turn, we have the possibility of learning to act differently. We do not have to look very hard to see that fear has made tremendous strides in the world; it infects us in peculiar ways and dominates us, often without our knowing it.

Having made these preliminary observations we need now to introduce our main character. Shall we have him wear a ski mask, forcing himself on a woman as she enters her apartment? Shall we have him be a doctor telling an unsuspecting patient that he has incurable lymphoma and will die in several weeks? Shall we have him be a soldier in Kosovo, spraying machine-gun fire into the center of a playground? Shall we have him be a corporate executive downsizing the company? Shall we have him be a legislator introducing a bill to eliminate Medicare? The choices are infinite.

Now, try to picture your greatest fear. Don't dwell on it for very long, just see what comes to mind when you focus for a moment on your greatest fear. This little exercise is not an experiment in visualization. The intent is just to help us begin to find a connection with the force of fear and what it may be doing. What appears may change from one day to another.

In all of the instances of fear that have been mentioned, notice that there is no context. It is quite likely that your own image of fear similarly lacks context. When you picture a fear, nothing of your own history, your personality, your level of soul development, your spiritual orientation, or the people who love and support you is present. In the list of fears above, we know nothing of the people involved, have no sense where and how they live, or of what they believe. And, in the absence of context, it is impossible to tell how different people would come through these circumstances. The imaginary exercise, nonetheless, is instructive. First, the exercise shows that when fear comes along, it strips away context. When increasingly more of the context of our lives has been removed, we use artificial barriers to protect ourselves. Such barriers—increased law enforcement, burglar alarms, the right to carry concealed weapons, drugs holding the promise of curing most diseases, political promises—often increase the fear they intend to remove.

If we fear crime, an answer might seem to be to put

more policemen on the street armed with more and more powerful weapons. If we fear illness, we may go to a doctor seeking a clean bill of health through elaborate tests and procedures. In all such instances, we dream of something outside of ourselves to take care of the problem of fear, but these outer controls merely add more fear to the world. In this sense, fear is a shape-shifter. When we think we have freed ourselves from fear, it shows up in the very means we're using to control it.

What defines many fearful situations is the sudden realization that we are no longer ourselves. If a robber accosts me at gunpoint, he has no notion of who I am. He doesn't care. He treats me not as an individual, not as a human being, but as a source of money. And, with gun in hand, he has the power, in an instant, to erase me from myself and make me exactly what he wants me to be— a cowering, compliant, shaking, powerless shell, nothing more than a dispenser of a wallet and jewelry. At that moment, I am no longer a psychologist, a writer, speaker, father, husband, teacher. I don't even have a name as far as the robber is concerned. A certain level of the self vanishes. If I have not gone deeper into myself in life than these externals, a situation of fear erodes my sense of identity.

The abstract word *victim* tries to cover this circumstance, but at that moment, I do not know myself as a victim. Rather, I find myself dominated by someone else's notion of who I am to them. The robber sees me as his supplier of money. The boss at the office may see me as a mere functionary. The enemy in international conflict may see us all as an evil to be destroyed.

The bodily reactions accompanying fear—dilation of the pupils, paleness, increased heartbeat, activation of the sympathetic nervous system—as well as psychological reactions such as anxiety, dread, cringing, fight or flight, and panic—are merely effects, and should not be confused with fear itself. Likewise, spiritual reactions, such as doubt, hesitancy, isolation, and loss of confidence, are also only effects. The primary action of fear is fragmentation. Once we are broken into parts, confusion sets in. We identify our fear as centered in one or more of these fragments and approach it as a bodily problem, a psychological problem, or a spiritual problem.

Fear removes the single center of our being, the only part of us capable of engaging it in the proper mode of struggle. The only way to approach fear is through the totality of our being, through the wholeness of being a person. If a medical doctor or a psychiatrist relies on medication as the way to relieve anxieties, phobias, and panic, the person is put at risk. If a psychologist or a counselor sees fear as a problem related to the way a person was treated in childhood, or as a complex, or as lack of self-esteem, the person is again put at risk. And if a spiritual advisor, priest, or spiritually inclined therapist sees fear as the result of sin, or a lack of connection with one's "higher self," or a turning away from religion, the centrality of the person as person has also been ignored.

Fear begins to infect the soul life when we are pulled out of ourselves. If we succumb, even in very subtle ways, to the false self that fear makes of us, we are from that moment living in fear, even though the initial bodily reactions subside. Further, the fact that we now experience the world as filled with fear means that we are continually subject to being who we are not, and, tragically, this can occur before we even have a sense of who we are and how we relate to the world.

Suppose I have a long-standing friendship with someone, and we are so closely connected that neither of us is concerned with asking, "Who am I in this relationship?" Then one day, this friend calls me on the telephone and tells me of a new work arrangement she has made with another person that directly competes with the work that I do. I suddenly fear that she has used our friendship to find out about how I succeed in my business. Her decision to work with the other person seems to nullify our friendship. A rift in the relationship has occurred. What really needs to be worked on is the friendship, and this would first require that I get to know the precise qualities and characteristics of the fear that has separated us. But, the rift may instead create a question, not about the friendship, but about myself. Have I done something wrong? Why am I not strong enough to let this person go? I feel so bad now that this relationship has dissolved; I am hurt, offended, maybe I will not be able to trust another person again. I realize that this reaction is way out of proportion. Finally, I go to a therapist to work on myself. With the therapist I discover that, due to circumstances of my early life, I am not secure in myself. We talk about fear, but it is taken to be only a symptom of the weakness of myself. As I get to know myself more completely, I am able to relate more freely to others, to enjoy relationships with them, and become more willing to let the other person be an autonomous self.

What is accomplished in this therapy, however, has more to do with the tactics of self-absorption, created by the tear in the fabric of connection and theorized about by the psychologist, than with finding the way to relatedness. I may learn to talk myself through difficult situations like the one I experienced with my former friend. I may learn to see the other person as a free and autonomous human being with individual likes and dislikes, and learn that these do not necessarily have anything to do with me. I may even learn that I can feel whole and complete without that person and that I do not have to protect myself by isolating myself. All of this certainly sounds like the development of a healthy sense of relatedness. What has actually happened, though, is that fear has taken me under its control. I have not learned more about how fear enters relatedness; rather, I have learned some tactics to avoid feeling fear. I have learned to take better care of myself, which is just a more sophisticated form of isolation. Under these circumstances, my development into a more soulful person through relationships has been stunted. True, I no longer experience fear when a friend or colleague severely disappoints me. A point of stability has been found in an insecure world. But it only looks as if fear has been resolved.

The difficulty is that in the process as described here, fear was considered to be "my" fear. My reaction to the presence of fear is mine, but fear, as anyone who has experienced it will say, takes possession of one, and cannot be considered as belonging to one as such. You can walk into a room and feel the fear all around. Or, you can sense fear existing between two individuals caught in a conflict. A whole country can be engulfed in fear.[3] In the earlier example, fear was also considered by the therapist to be the result of an inadequate sense of self, though if we look more deeply, the focus in the therapy was ego identity. The fear prompted reassessing this identity in therapy, and actually created more self-centeredness and, in that sense, more isolation. The current of my relationships with others has now become restricted to a sense of how to take care of myself. Now, fear can do its work unnoticed. Fear is what keeps me highly alert to the necessity of taking care of myself. However, it no longer looks like fear but rather like being "more together."

While fear cannot be tricked, it is possible to avoid being tricked by it, to avoid doing its work by having enough presence of mind to spot its disguises, the various pretenses under which it operates. First, we have to come to be able to recognize fear as an alien presence. It does not belong to us, although our reactions to it make it seem like it is ours. But it exists before our reactions to it do. It claws at us. We may dispel it for a moment by thinking that it is only our imagination. But, after a few seconds, it reasserts itself as a wordless threat. There is no physical trace of its presence; it cannot be located spatially, beside, or above, or within, or over in the corner, or hovering in midair. But it is unmistakably present, a force of its own.

It is an illusion to think that we can handle fear by becoming more controlling—of our lives, of our relationships, of our situations, of our world. We treat the symptoms, thinking they are the fear. It goes into hiding by appearing to be one with our personality, creating different forms of ego identity as a camouflage. I may learn to think of myself as being in charge of my relationships. Or I may view myself as a wonderful protector of all the dangers my family might encounter—the different forms of ego identity I adopt will depend on the nature of the fear. As we shall see later, fear actually creates many different false senses of the self, each of which conforms to our personality.

In each instance of fear we encounter, the task we are confronted with is to shatter the pretenses, which are intensely cunning. Under the guise of strengthening the self, for example, fear casts blame for our weaknesses on what our parents did to us or failed to do, on the traumas we have undergone, the abuses suffered. In fact, the tragic things that have happened to us can be seen as the cause of our weaknesses, or they can be seen as gateways leading to deeper and more conscious soul life. If we view the difficulties of life as weaknesses, fear has found a hiding place to do its work. If we view the difficulties as gateways, we avoid thinking we have gotten rid of fear, and instead develop strength of soul to balance out any fears that may be present.

From Self to Person

Our humanity comes not from a complete absence of fear, but from a courageous, unending struggle with it.

The small but absolutely necessary domain of human freedom is to be found here—in freely choosing to enter this ongoing struggle. And the intention of this struggle is not to achieve absolute victory, but to grow in our humanity.

Here's an instance of someone willfully entering the struggle with fear instead of being controlled by it. Alan, a seventy-year-old man, simple-natured but full of life and energy and interest in everything around him, came to a doctor because he was passing blood in his urine. He felt well and had never been seriously ill before. A physical examination revealed that his right kidney was enlarged. These two symptoms, along with his age, strongly suggested that there was a malignant tumor on the right kidney. To confirm this diagnosis the doctor told Alan that he would have to be hospitalized for further tests.

When the doctor told Alan that because there was a strong possibility of cancer he would have to go to the hospital, he refused. He wanted to stay at home. The doctor told him that the ailment was most likely very serious, and that if the tumor was malignant the kidney would have to be removed. If he did have a malignant tumor, he would almost certainly suffer a great deal and die a miserable death. He asked Alan to consider those around him, his wife and children, his friends. Why stay home and die instead of having the disease treated and, at least, gain more time? Alan still refused. He refused to be taken from the house where he had lived, worked, and raised his children. He refused to leave who he knew he was and be put into the alien world of the hospital. He did not intend to just go home and wait to die. He would go there and take care of himself in the most natural ways possible. He was satisfied with his life, grateful for his seventy years.

It's important to distinguish between the immediacy of bodily reactions and the sort of fear that infects soul life. Alan certainly must have felt fear at hearing the doctor's pronouncement. His heart speeded up; he probably felt great anxiety and wanted to run, to escape. But he did not allow himself to be taken over by fear.

Alan also must have found himself suddenly without his identity. But his inner resources did not allow anything else to usurp, beyond momentarily, who he knew himself to be. He did not react to fear and go along with a treatment that did not seem right for him. He was able to stand up to the urgings of the doctor. This story is most interesting because while the doctor seemed to be offering Alan life, Alan instinctively knew that he was being offered not life, but fear. Somewhere, from deep within, he knew that to be taken off to the hospital, dressed in a skimpy white gown, put into a room with strangers, poked and probed, drugged, opened up, and submitted to radiation treatment would mean that he would never again belong to himself. Moreover, he instinctively knew that he would never recover from this separation from himself. For others, such a recovery might indeed be possible, and for those people, submitting to treatment would be the right option.

This man faced his situation, and faced himself: thus, this is not a case of denial. His soul was free from fear. He did not relinquish himself when confronted with fear, not because his sense of identity was stronger, more developed, more mature than most, but, I suggest, because he had, through years of living—though indeed it must have been living in a rather extraordinary way—arrived at a certain degree of selflessness. He was his home, his family, his surroundings, his friends, though not in any literal way, of course. When I said earlier that Alan must be someone with inner resources, "inner" does not refer to things located somewhere inside this individual. Quite to the contrary, inner resources here have to do with the way this person is interwoven with the world, with the kinds of qualities this person had come to experience, not in himself alone, but in conjunction with everyone around him.[4] We can imagine his home as filled with warmth, care, memories; his family as emanating respect for him; his surroundings as perhaps quite simple, a life of work, friends, values.

People like Alan, who have a sense of their presence in the world as real, are not living without fear. But fear cannot dominate them because of the fabric of relations that exist between them and the world, of which fear is but one of the threads. When, however, the threads of this fabric begin to unravel—when the world becomes more unreal than real, or when an inner experience such as a powerful dream or an overwhelming emotion takes one over—then a hole in the fabric of relations occurs, and a question mark arises. This question mark can be the wake-up call that pushes us, not in quest of the self directly but toward deepening the sense of our vital connections with the world.

What gives fear the potential to awaken us to new possibilities of existence is the fact that there is *no escape*. Fear cannot be put outside, into some corner of the world, fenced off, and labeled as the Fear Prison, so that we know where it is and can avoid it. Rather, we are called to work with fear, to get to know it intimately, never imagining that it can be our friend, but also not making it into our enemy. Approaching fear as an enemy forces us into fearful means to try to get rid of it, which paradoxically only strengthens its presence.

Fear can bring us into contact with capacities we did not even know we had. A first intimation of these capacities comes with the realization that it is not possible to get rid of fear, but it is possible to gradually transform it.

Transform it into what? Fear can be shaped into capacities of soul that can bring the forces of love into the world. Love works to cancel fear because love is a force of connection and attraction, while fear is a force of separation and division.[5] For this transformation to come about we have to approach fear alchemically rather than scientifically. When we imagine that fear is the effect of a cause that, if found and eliminated, will no longer control us, we are thinking scientifically. We proceed alchemically, however, when we approach fear as a basic substance of our being, and of the world itself. Our task will be to discover how to make gold out of this dung— the gold being a whole human being who is increasingly less fragmented by fear.

Finding words to adequately describe humanness is not easy; perhaps the word *humanness* is too abstract. What we struggle to become is a complete person. Abstractly, we could say that a person is the undivided unity of body, soul, and spirit, fully woven into a fabric of relations with others and the world, uninhibited in expression. We all recognize the countenance of the *person*; there is a radiance, a glow, a warmth that leads us to feel more of who we truly are. We feel that nothing is being hidden, that this individual is true, genuine, not protecting or guarding anything. We feel that such an individual is not out to get something from us. We certainly do not feel any fear emanating from this person, which does not mean the individual no longer experiences fear but that he or she is not a carrier of it. We can be very sure that, far more than being just a pleasant personality, such an individual has struggled with many demons, both inner and outer, and has come to discover the inviolable region of the heart.

Freeing the soul from fear means participating in fear, not naively and not like a sheep being led to slaughter, but with the greatest intensity of consciousness and attention we are able to muster. Heightening of consciousness is involved, but it is here inseparable from the pain that goes with any expansion of awareness and does not have as its aim mastery over what threatens us. This approach demands increased attentiveness to the particularities of our experience, which can come about only by becoming acutely conscious to the realm of the senses—more open, more awake, more alive, precisely in those situations where freedom would seem to be offered by escaping, by going numb. Even more, what is here required is the development of an intense effort of sympathetic insight, penetration into the reasons and causes of fear, and even into the minds of those who may be the perpetrators. Developing such insight is very difficult because it must be done without nurturing even a trace of sentimentality, which would excuse the actions of the perpetrators. And, equally, insight must be developed without a trace of sentimentality toward ourselves, without falling into victim mentality.

Going through this process brings gradual but quite radical changes in us. Layer by layer, previous conditioning is removed, and with it all the mistaken hopes we have lived by for years and years. In all of us, such conditioning comes about through parents, schooling, religion, law, convention, tradition, and the civilization and culture within which we live. Everything that has given us a sense of certitude in life is subject to being taken away, including what seem to be, on the surface, our very best qualities and attributes. We get a chance, indeed, to see these characteristics for the masks they are, appreciate them for what they have provided, and at the same time see how they have kept us on the surface and concerned with protecting our own needs and desires. The stripping process then gradually lays bare the many layers of our subconscious, where we have an opportunity to face the not-so-delightful aspects of the emotions, passions, drives—what Jung speaks of as the shadow elements of our personality. We get to face our own pettiness and self-centeredness, but also the strengths we did not know we have, and power we might be hesitant to look at. Finally, we arrive at the nakedness of soul.

The way is perilous, for at any point, at any revealed

layer, the opportunity exists for fear to make use of what is uncovered. Here is an example: Carol, a member of one of our workshops, came to discover that she had built a life on the importance of reputation. Now, this seemed to be a good thing. It certainly need not be false or harmful. After all, if one has grown up, as she did, in the tradition of a fine, aristocratic southern family in which the father, the grandfather, and everyone going back several generations were all upright citizens in the community, in which service to the community, the church, and the local university brought much good, then it is understandable why she would be conditioned to act in a similar manner. It is here, however, around the layer of conditioning that says one should act a certain way, that fear will gather and try to take control. Carol constantly felt that she had to do things that were respectable. She put aside her own deep interests in learning, writing, and teaching in order to do charitable, civic, and organizational work that would be honored by the community. If she failed in any of these endeavors, she felt intense fear. If she did the least bit that might stain her reputation, she experienced great anxiety. She even found herself doing things to maintain that reputation, no matter the cost to others. She made sure that she was placed in charge of events, got into power struggles with people who were her friends, and blamed others when things did not go precisely as she wanted. For Carol, coming free of fear meant stripping away each of these levels of conditioning, one by one, going through intense fear as she became conscious of each layer.

To take another example, a person may be thrown immediately into the deepest levels of the subconscious by being subjected to a trauma, such as rape. Such trauma often strips away all our protection in one fell swoop. Under such a condition of nakedness of soul, the person may experience upsurges of the worst sort, such as uncontrollable anger or depression. One who is made vulnerable and tossed into the midst of the unknown can be taken over by fear and driven to despair. Tremendous effort must be exerted not to cover such wounds with new layers of conditioning. The appearance of fear and trembling announces to us that another layer has been removed and helps us realize how much we live in illusion.

Fear is the only thing that can eat through the cast-iron layers of the false self and take us to our core where, if it is met with intensified soul consciousness rather than given in to, its transformation into virtue can begin. We need only to call to mind the stories of individuals who lived through the experiences of war, or concentration camps, who were confined and tortured for their struggles against political oppression, who have met the most horrifying illness, who struggle with the effects of all sorts of abuse. The corrosive effects of fear can bring about a free and open soul life, oriented toward care and service, and a deep feeling and knowing of love; it can also make us into mere shells of human beings. The difference seems to lie in whether, in the presence of fear, we open more to the soul or become closed to the depths of our existence.

Developing Soul Capacities to Balance Fear

Fear erodes our natural human capacities. For example, if we become afraid of others, our natural capacity for trust is eroded. Or if we have gone through some kind of physical trauma, our natural capacity to be open in our senses becomes constricted. The capacities that fear erodes must then be developed through conscious inner work. By strengthening our inner resources and making them less penetrable, the various fears we encounter can be weakened. A number of meditative exercises are included in the following chapters, and each exercise has a similar form. First, you are asked to make an inner image of a particular sort, depending on the kind of fear being worked with. Then, it is necessary to hold the image, to stabilize it so that it does not turn into something else. After holding the image for a while, it is deliberately dissolved, and you are to focus on the inner emptiness.[6] The process develops an inner strength of soul. It takes soul strength to form an inner image. It also takes strength to stabilize and hold the image. Once an image is formed and stabilized in this way, it then takes further strength to erase the image and to stay present to the emptiness. In this manner, new soul capacities are formed, capacities directly oriented toward balancing the presence of fear.

As an entry into the kind of image-work employed in the following chapters, you might try making an inner image of a simple object, such as a stone. Find an ordinary stone and observe it for a few minutes, turning it over in your hand. Then, close your eyes and make an inner image of this stone. The intention is to make an image that pictures the stone exactly as you saw it. Notice where the image seems to appear. If it appears in the region of the eyes, as if you were looking at it, then that is a mental image, which is more like having an idea of the stone rather than a deeper, more living image. If you have only a mental image of the stone you will see only the surface facing you. You begin to have more of a soul-image of the object when a feeling of the whole of the object appears; you may not see the whole visually, but the quality of the whole will be present. The intention is to stabilize the image, to hold it steady for as long as possible. It may begin to move; if so, bring it back to center. If it begins to fade, exercise a gentle act of will to bring it back. You may also find that the image begins to take on new characteristics. It may begin to become animated, or you may start to think about something associated with the stone, perhaps where you found it, and before you know it, you are off into a thought or a fantasy. Once you recognize this is happening, return to the image.

After holding the image steady for a few minutes, extinguish it and be present to the void for as long as possible without letting any other thought or image enter. You may also notice the presence of fear or some amount of anxiety. The presence of fear interferes with the capacity to concentrate. The real aim of the exercise, however, is to become familiar with what must be done to make and hold an image. It is not enough to remember the stone you observed; you have to make an image of it. The act of making the image takes a force of will. But at the same time, in order for the image to be present, there must be receptivity to what presents itself. These two qualities have to be perfectly balanced. If the act of will is too strong, then the image will be distorted in some fashion. If the will is not strong enough to hold the image, then the image will start to have an autonomy of its own; you may suddenly see sparks or lights, or the stone will turn into an image of the whole earth—or any number of other possibilities.

A second aim of the exercise concerns the moment of extinguishing the image and trying to stay with the emptiness. By emptiness I mean that, for a short while, no thought, image, or memory enters consciousness. This part of the exercise strengthens the capacity of the will. You will notice that it takes a force of concentration to stay with the emptiness, and that this concentration can even be felt in the body. You are using will to maintain the emptiness. At first, you may find it difficult to stay with the void for more than a few seconds. Other images may intrude, or thoughts, or you may feel somewhat tired. With repeated effort the period of time becomes longer, though it is never easy.

To make a vivid image and then to extinguish that image makes an opening, a place of not-knowing that needs to be strongly held as a center of operations. This center of not-knowing is the one secure place where the forces of fear cannot enter. Not-knowing does not mean doubt, for doubt is the open door for the forces of fear. Doubt makes a space for confusion, and confusion leads to full-blown skepticism, a sure sign that negative forces have taken hold. Not-knowing, however, also does not mean unconsciousness. This quality of not-knowing is held in full clarity of consciousness and can be attained only by the process of making inner images, extinguishing them, holding the inner emptiness, and listening to it. What begins to come in the inner emptiness is a quality of feeling, a feeling of protection, an inner surety that one can meet and engage fear without becoming totally lost.

Developing the imagination is of utmost importance as a starting point for launching into more detailed considerations of fear. In the absence of such a starting point, anything said about fear runs the very great risk of producing more fear. The exercise suggested above is an important variation of what we do when faced with anxiety of any sort. We try to find a central place within that is calm. We may practice deep breathing, center ourselves, hold onto something secure, try to find something familiar. If we look at each of these practices individually, something quite interesting is revealed.

In finding a place of inner calmness, one seeks respite from onslaughts internally. In holding onto something secure or familiar, one seeks this respite externally. And with deep breathing, one tries to establish a unity between what is outside and what is inside. Air outside is taken in, and what is inside is then expelled. If breathing becomes rhythmic, timed in the right way, an inside-outside continuity is established. The exercises in the following chapters extend the usual process of restoring calm to the realm of the imagination, to the whole domain of soul life, so that experiences of fear that are more than fleeting can be worked with in healthy ways.

Fear, as it eats away the layers of our outer and even our inner being, comes to a central core of fire, which can only be called a fire of love, a mysterious fire that we ourselves do not ignite or even maintain, but which glows eternally in the heart of our being. While it may come about by following one or another of the spiritual traditions, this fire needs to be kindled by engagement with fear itself. We can learn to utilize the poison of fear to deepen soul, develop soul and spirit consciousness, and strengthen the fiery forces of creative love.

Who we are in the depth of our being does not consist of some central substance, an invisible entity submersed somewhere within the folds of our physical body, persisting despite all changes of circumstance. Are we not, at the very core of our being, more like a burning flame of light? The metaphor of the flame, at any rate, reveals an inner core of mystery, something beyond ordinary conception, something capable of bringing warmth and light into the world as well as incinerating fear. As our exploration of fear continues, this metaphor of the central flame of our being will be our guide.

CHAPTER 2

The Body in Fear

Fear brings terrible discomfort to the body. Indeed, we probably could not physically endure living with the constant presence of fear. Anyone living for an extended period of time in a fearful situation begins to be numb, but the body, even when numb, continues to be affected. Strengthening the soul against such effects means looking at not just the immediate physiological accompaniments of fear but also the changes wrought in the senses most associated with giving us our feelings of bodily being. It also means finding ways of preserving the fullness of bodily life when we are beset with fear and, in so doing, assuring the continuance of the radiant life of the soul.

The various senses can be considered portals to the realm of the soul. Everything that we experience—

particularly fearful experience—reverberates into the body and continues to do so long after it is conscious. Freeing the soul from fear first of all means keeping the body vitally responsive to the world, free from numbness, even in the presence of factors that would effectively narrow and constrict relationship with the world.

The boundaries of soul life do not end at the skin. In the ordinary way we live, our being is much more pliant than the perceptible physical organism that we identify as our body. We live constantly beyond our physical being, in the extension of the body's subtle and supple boundaries into its surroundings. A blind person walking with a cane, for example, feels the tip of the cane at the point of contact with the sidewalk, and his sense of touch extends to that region. When we reach out to pick up a glass of water in front of us, the action is not merely mechanical. A subtle aspect of our consciousness is already there, grasping the glass, even before we reach it with our physical organism. As we move around in the world, we do not perceive the world as "over there"; we are in the world, belong to it, are part of it, and it is part of us.[1] Taken together, the physical body along with the continual extension of its more subtle aspects into the wider world can be termed our "soul-body."

The boundaries of the soul-body do not coincide with those of the physical body. If they did, we would experience the world as very strange indeed; it would be something akin to looking at our surroundings as projected on a screen before us. When we experience fear, the surrounding world begins to recede from our intimate engagement, and we become spectators. In more extreme states of fear, the world appears like a flat surface spread out before us.

Although it's difficult to describe the way we experience our environment, we have no difficulty whatsoever living it. While we are always bodily in the world, we do not lose ourselves "out there"; we still feel the location of our body as "with us." We are "here" and "there" at the same time. The aspect of our body as "here" certainly has more of a quality of solidity, while our being-with the things of our surroundings is a much more subtle kind of engagement.

To experience the unified field of your body and the world, you have to experiment a little; try to become aware, for a few moments, of the flexible polarity of bodily life. As I sit here looking at a lamp, it appears to be in front of me, thus locating my body as here and the lamp as over there. But until the moment I considered it, I did not experience the lamp as "over there"; I merely experienced a unified perceptual field that included my body within the awareness of the lamp, and the lamp within my bodily awareness. The field is what occurs between our body and the objects we perceive, and it encompasses both. The physics of fields has shown that the dynamic relation between things is more primary than the objects that form the relationship. Perception also takes place as a field, and only our conceptual thinking neatly divides the perceiver from the perceived.

Of course, boundaries do exist between us and the surrounding world, but such boundaries vary all the time according to what we are doing and our focus of attention—the presence of fear being the principal thing that disturbs this flexible boundary. When we're afraid, the soul-body contracts, producing a strong polarity where there once was unity. We feel ourselves as more isolated from and threatened by the world. The body-world unity becomes more like two polarized objects facing each other. In extreme instances, the contraction can be felt as a jolt, a shock, in which suddenly a sharp boundary arises, with us on one side of the boundary and the hostile presence of fear on the other side. The snapping into place of this boundary forms an access point through which fear can then enter deeply into us. At such moments, everything around us begins to be perceived as a threat. If, for example, I am walking down a dark street at night and see a shadowy figure step out of an alley, I no longer comfortably belong with my surroundings. I do not fear just the shadowy figure—everything becomes a signature of that shadow. A slight sound becomes the sign that the shadowy figure has just stepped on a twig; a movement of leaves on a tree becomes further evidence of its existence. The night itself becomes a harbinger of dread.

As long as the threshold between our body and the surrounding world remains flexible, we resist fears because another force pervades our intimacy with the world. This force is the presence of love. As long as the world appears familiar to us, welcoming, beckoning, embracing us as an intimate partner, seeming to invite us to participate with it, we are in the presence of a quality within the world that can rightly be called love. I define love here simply as the force of connection, in contradistinction to fear as the force of antipathy. Love, too, belongs to a wider reality than our own little existence. You can feel it when you walk into a room where love has visited. You can sense love going back and forth between people. Much more will be said later concerning love's capacity to dissolve fears. But we need a conception of love that's wider than being something that exists between ourselves and others, or ourselves and God.

When we become more aware of the quality of love in the world, we experience the world as sacred. We feel sacredness most vividly at the farthest reaches of our soul-body, when we are stretched to the limit, which usually occurs as we encounter something new and beautiful. Think of approaching the Grand Canyon for the first time, or seeing a comet in the sky, or coming upon a small violet flower growing out of the crack in a rock above timberline, or visiting Chartres Cathedral, or gazing at a Cézanne painting. Such beauty powerfully draws us beyond our immediate body and into what we perceive. At such liminal places, transformation can take place; we become different, more than we imagined.

The moment fear strikes, on the other hand, it is as if our body contracts. We strongly feel the physical processes of our body. We become acutely aware of our breathing, of the racing of the blood, of the pounding of the heart, sweating, or of the urge to urinate. At this very moment it is as if fear crosses the invisible boundary between ourselves and the world and enters our body. We then feel afraid, and the fear seems to be our own, but it is not; fear has invaded us. Fear has stolen our soul and begins reducing us to our physical nature.

Some people can rebound from such experiences of fear rather readily, while others cannot. Those who do not rebound suffer from trauma. The key factor involves strength of soul. Stealing the soul from the body means that the capacity of imaginative engagement with the world fades. When we suffer the effects of fears, we begin to imagine all sorts of things that are not present— dream life may go wild, presenting us with nightly images of terror from which the only escape is waking up in a sweat. But this kind of imagination has a very different quality from the imagination lived in conjunction with the world. Depth psychology has tended to see the sort of vivid imaginary life that occurs when we are living in crisis as stemming from the unconscious and consisting of archetypal imagery. The images themselves do not seem connected with events or experiences during waking life. Delving more closely into the invasion of fears into the body, however, shows us something quite different.

Fear acts on the very organs of the body, affecting them direly. Even after the immediate physiological effects of fear subside, the organs remain affected. A wound has been inflicted.[2] If you bruise the palm of your hand, the pain subsides after a few moments. If you then grasp something where the skin has been rubbed away, it hurts. Similarly, even though they may not show actual physical damage, the wounds inflicted on the organs of the body by fear are sore and tender, particularly in their soul element. The world becomes experienced in a painful way. Now fear works from the inside, restricting the flow of soul energy into the world. Vivid imaginations of being trapped, bound, tortured, chased, can arise either as waking fantasies or in the form of dreams. Depth psychology, because it focuses only on the psyche and not on the whole person, interprets such images in terms of archetypal content. While there may be a more vivid image content after someone has been frightened, such imagery is intimately bound up with bodily conditions.

When fears become incorporated in the body, the way we sense our body is the first and most significant domain where alteration of sensing occurs. While there are twelve senses (Rudolf Steiner enumerates them as touch, the life sense, movement, balance, smell, taste, the temperature sense, vision, hearing, the speech sense, the thought sense, and the sense of individuality), the first four give us our experience of our own body, each in different ways. Through these senses we experience how we feel, how we are in our bodily being, how we stand and walk, lie and sit. We do not experience the outer world through these four senses, but rather our body in relation to what goes on around us.

The invasion of the body by fears also sets up subtle ways in which fears begin to shape the way we perceive, think, and act in the world. A hypersensitivity to the world develops. We begin to feel that we cannot move safely in the world. The senses connected with immediate sensations of the body are most affected—touch, the life sense, the sense of movement, and the sense of balance. Rudolf Steiner was the first to understand the function of these senses as directly related to experiencing the body rather than sensing the surrounding world.[3] When we live in fear, our body is most immediately affected. However, we adjust to living in fear and then do not realize that we have become closed to the fuller reality of the world due to the sensory constrictions of the body.

The Touch of Fear

The invasion of fear into our corporeal existence particularly affects the capacities of the senses. The narrowing of sensing coordinates with constriction of soul; therefore, consciously working to free sensing from fear goes hand in hand with freeing soul life from fear.

We have come to understand our bodies according to the medical-scientific concept of the body. The medical view of the body is based on the anatomy of the corpse and on the physiology of a dismembered human body. From this point of view, the senses are the physiological organs and processes linked with the brain to produce sense experience. However, we do not live in our bodies in such a fashion. The living body is an open field, a locus for the convergence of relationships—with the world, with other people, with the soul realms, with the spirit realms. Sensing occurs in this open field, between our body and these extended surroundings. Consequently, we must invite soul and spirit back into our own living being in order to experience the fullness of embodiment. In this way, we can regain a soul-sense of embodiment. Soul and spirit are not invisible entities lurking around as ghosts in a machine; the body, through and through, is ensouled and inspirited.

When we touch something, we ordinarily feel that we perceive the qualities of the object touched. If I touch a metal handrail, I sense something nonyielding, and it feels quite different from touching a wooden handrail. Touch seems to give us the presence of the object at hand. Closer observation, however, shows that this perception is not quite correct. When we touch something metal or something wood, the object presses in on us; this pressing-in results in a change, even if very slight, in body position, a change detected through the sense of balance. I can also see the object and discern that it is metal and not wood. Metal feels cold, while wood feels more neutral in temperature. I also reach out to grasp the railing, and thus the sense of movement becomes involved. If we try to attend to the sense of touch alone for a moment, putting aside what we experience of the object through the other senses, we sense only the body meeting with a resistance. The object presses my skin inward, and I discover the border between my body and the world.

The experience of touch is not limited to the skin. When the bladder fills, for example, a kind of pressure or pulling sensation will be felt. If an inner organ swells, a similar pulling sensation occurs. The pulsing of blood in the fingertips also belongs to the realm of touch. In all instances, touch conveys an experience of boundaries, of bodily borders. The border may be between my hand and an object, my body and something that is not my body, an organ of the body in relation to the whole of the body, or even the blood in relation to the rest of the body. The exact area of sensation is experienced. When we take a step, the pressure of the shoe meets the ground in a particular place. Often, the experience of touch is the experience of location. If I am lying on a warm, sandy beach with my eyes closed, and an ant crawls up my arm, touch locates the exact position of the ant. In all cases, the sensation of touch gives us the sense of our body, not as an object but as a living being.

When fear affects the body, the sense of touch changes. For example, someone who has experienced physical abuse undergoes a severe change in the sense of touch, resulting in a terrible simultaneous need for and a fear of touch. Such change can also occur after undergoing painful surgery or a serious accident. The body, now living in a more contracted state, experiences ongoing anxiety. This feels like a pulling or a tearing all over the body; it is like being touched by something, though what touches you remains invisible. This powerful sensation interferes with the capacity to think or to feel. We may get goose pimples or our hair may stand on end; we may break out in a sweat, start trembling uncontrollably, our teeth may chatter, our heart may thump, and we may even have diarrhea. But, since the particular fear that brought about this contraction may have passed and be long forgotten, or may not even have been noticed, the state of anxiety is most often interpreted as an inner, psychological difficulty. The anxious person goes off to the doctor to receive a tranquilizer or to a therapist for treatment. The whole world, in fact, becomes structured around trying to quiet our anxiety. We may feel that new clothes will help, or a lavish meal, or entertainment, or a thousand other distractions. In this manner, fears remain free to roam the world because we have been tricked into taking fears as our personal psychological difficulties rather than as having been touched by the objective presence of fear.

When the sense of touch functions in a healthy way, we instinctively feel a numinous quality in everything that surrounds us. Because our senses are so assaulted and overstimulated, we become conscious of this quality primarily in relation to the natural world. However, if we slow down a bit and give close attention to our immediate surroundings, something of this numinous quality can be brought back to life. The beautiful texture of a brick wall, a stately tree in the middle of cement surroundings, the look of a person we happen to walk by—just about anything radiates depth when we are open to what is present. Touch gives the experience of being a body, of being other than the surrounding world, but it also offers the possibility of being in intimate relation with an ineffable holy presence in the world.

The presence of fear, when it is strong, disrupts our ability to sense the numinous quality within the things of the world. What we previously experienced quite naturally must now become a conscious work. We are now called to work out of our own soul realm, to find and experience numinosity in an inner way, and then to return this presence to the world rather than keeping it for ourselves exclusively. Instead of directly trying to relieve our anxieties, the objective is to perceive anxiety as an indicator of the severing of the deep, numinous qualities of the world and of those around us. If this connection can be restored, then anxiety will also cease naturally. Tranquilizers only cover anxiety. Therapy can be helpful in coming to experience an inner quality of divine presence, and thus assuage anxieties, but it typically does not provide ways of bringing a balance to the presence of fears in the world. Shifting our imagination of the world may be more useful. Think of the world as a sacred place, a temple. Work at strengthening this image so that it becomes an everyday reality. Before suggesting any further ways to achieve this balance, we will describe fears in relation to the other senses of our body.

Fear in the Life Sense

Touch is not the only sense through which we experience bodily life. Another sense affected by fear is the life sense, the bodily experience of our own vitality. Sensory physiology and psychology have not yet recognized this sense, though it is something quite evident.

When the life sense operates undisturbed, we are hardly aware of its presence. When we wake up in the morning and feel great, the experience is an actual sense experience. We sense a feeling of bodily well-being. We are much more aware of this sense when things do not go so well with our body. The feeling of being tired, or exhausted, or hungry, or thirsty—these are sense experiences. We do not hear or smell the tiredness, but we do perceive it, and the sense that does this perceiving is the life sense. Through this sense we experience the wholeness of our body, so that each of us feels the body as "my body." We do not experience our body as a conglomeration of organs along with a skeletal structure, but as a whole.

As fear affects us, we not only become filled with anxieties but also find ourselves more uncomfortable in our body—it begins to feel more like an object we have to lug around. We may feel tired for no reason, filled with an ongoing sense of exhaustion. A dim but pervading sense of depression accompanies us all the time. Unlocatable pains, stirrings of hunger—such sensations indicate a discomfort with the body. We may find ourselves eating to try to restore comfort, taking medication, sleeping too little or too much. Such measures may alleviate discomfort, but they do not restore a sense of well-being in the body; they merely obscure discomfort and allow us to perform our duties, but our body is not enthusiastic about being in the world.

These kinds of symptoms often indicate the ongoing presence of fears we have come to live with, despite our not being conscious that they are present. Often, spending time in the natural world brings about a renewal of vitality, of the life sense. This renewal, however, is not simply due to getting away from the stresses of everyday work and life; it has more to do with the body reengaging with the wider world. The key to overcoming fears is to find ways of strengthening soul life so that such reengagement can occur no matter where we are. Nature can be healing, not simply because it is nature but because what we sense there is not hard, rigid, static. The natural world has much more rhythmic motion, such as the movement of the leaves in the wind, the flow of a stream, the grandeur of the mountains raising toward the sky, the gentle spread of a valley. We are not overstimulated in the natural world. Once we realize that it is not nature, per se, but the forms and qualities of sense experience in nature that restore the life sense, we can in fact develop simple exercises for keeping our body flexible in relation to our surroundings.

Fear in Movement and Balance

The disruption of the four bodily senses by fear not only intensifies feelings of anxiety and dims our vital interest of bodily participation in the world but also brings about a disruption of the will. The capacities to move out into the world, to have goals, ideals, aspirations, and to get things done with enthusiasm and interest are aspects of the will. We typically think of the will as having to do with an aspect of the mind, but the forces of the will also take place within the soul-body. For example, I can have the idea and the desire to play major-league baseball, but the act of the will through which it can be accomplished takes place through the body. I have to go out there and play ball. The disruption of the will becomes most apparent with the bodily sense of movement. The system for the sense of movement is the musculature of the body. When

I move my arm, there is an inner experience of that movement, a sensing of the motion. This sense perceives not only large movements of the body but also very fine and subtle ones—the in-and-out movement of the chest while breathing, the motion of the neck and head as they turn, the movement of the eyes.

With the sense of touch we become conscious of the physical limits of our body. With the life sense we experience, in an inner way, the liveliness of bodily existence. With the sense of movement we perceive the different parts of the body in relation to each other. With this sense we do not perceive the movement of other bodies or objects, but those of our own body. The sensations of standing, sitting, walking, running, writing, blinking our eyes, or following the motion of something with our eyes are all experiences of the sense of movement. These perceptions, in relation to each other, give us the experience of the mobility of bodily life, the experience of moving around through the world while retaining a coherent sense of ourselves. This is the bodily basis for the experience of freedom.

When the body lives more in fear and anxiety, the experience of freedom fades from actual sensation. Fears invade the body and constrict the sense of movement. And with this constriction, we no longer know where we are going, what we are oriented toward, or how to get there. The sense of movement gives a bodily basis for freedom as well as a bodily basis for a feeling of purpose. Another quality connected with the sense of movement is joy. It is the sense of movement that keeps us from experiencing our body or the environment as a burden. When there is freedom of movement, we feel joy. Joy is a kind of liberation, a release, a state of being. To the extent we do not feel free, do not experience a sense of purpose, do not feel the presence of joy, it is because our body has been invaded by fears, and our soul movements and bodily sensations have become tight and restricted.

Balance is the fourth sense that gives the experience of our body. It allows us to experience the position of the body in relation to the space and things around us. The organ for the perception of balance lies in the inner ear, within the three semicircular canals. Through this sense we distinguish up from down, right from left, front from back. Balance is a primary sense of orientation, although many might think that vision alone suffices to orient us. The sense of balance, the inner orientation we always carry with us, gives us the possibility of ordering and orienting all other sense impressions. The sense of balance brings us into harmony with our surroundings.

When we lose our balance, the senses of life, movement, and touch are affected. We feel nauseated and perceive a disruption of the life sense; movement may become erratic; we search for something to touch so that we may once again experience our body. A specific sensation accompanies the loss of balance—the sensation of giddiness. We sometimes even feel an attraction to this sensation. Children love to spin around, faster and faster, until they fall down, delighting in the dizziness of the world spinning around. Adolescents seek another form of giddiness, often brought about through loud, riotous music that harshly penetrates into the very bones of the body, drawing them down into the underworld—a different sense of giddiness.

The sense of balance maintains the right relationship between lightness and gravity; this is what it means to be a human being on the Earth, beneath the sky. Losing our balance can send us in either of two directions—floating off into space, losing the quality of gravity, or sinking down into the subnatural world, the underworld, losing the quality of lightness of being. Thus, vertigo can take two directions. The feeling of fear strongly affects our sense of balance, throwing us into an ongoing vertigo, even if we do not experience constant dizziness. Under such conditions, soul life is also affected, making inner steadiness difficult.

The exact mechanisms of the organ of balance are quite complicated but are well known to physiology. Besides the more obvious ways indicated above, much more subtle states of imbalance can gradually insinuate themselves into the body. An initial symptom of imbalance is a buzzing in the ears, which indicates that the pulsating blood is disrupting the stillness of the ear's inner labyrinth. The beat of the pulse overcomes the rhythm of breathing and moves into the foreground. As the pulse of the blood gains the upper hand, there is a gradual loss of balance.

A more subtle way in which we are thrown out of balance is in disturbances to the rhythm of breathing. The connections with fear now become obvious. When fears inhabit the body, a first indication that this has happened appears in the change in the rhythm of the breath. We certainly know that a strong presence of fear results in symptoms of loss of balance such as nausea, vomiting, or even fainting. Once fears install themselves in the body, more gradual changes of breathing occur, and balance is lost in a more imperceptible manner, a little bit at a time.

The capacity to feel ourselves situated in our body, oriented in the world, has yet a more profound dimension. There is a sense of balance within the soul that can be described as inner peace, an inner equilibrium. This constitutes how we feel ourselves to be continuous, enduring beings. I feel I am the same person today as I was yesterday; changes certainly occur, even at very deep levels, but a central core of permanence remains. This core is the experience of ourselves as spirit. When this bodily sense of our spiritual being becomes disrupted, we lose this deep, inner feeling of who we are, and our spiritual identity is jeopardized. The capacity to bring the gifts of true individuality into the world is dimmed. We then operate more from the mass consciousness of the popular culture, expressed as egotistic individualism, rather than from our spiritual core.

People do all kinds of things these days to find ways of sensing spirit, not realizing that spirit lives here where we are, in and with our body. Such spirit-seeking can be seen as a symptom, an indication that the body, inhabited by fear, has lost its orientation.

Reducing Bodily Fear

The constriction of our bodily senses prevents a healthy, ongoing flow between the inner world of our soul life, reaching out to the world in desires, and the wonders of the outer world, gently reaching the soul through the portals of the senses. A simple exercise, done for no more than five minutes each day, can help keep the relation of soul and sensing vital and dynamic so that fear cannot come to have permanent effects on our bodily being. The meditation explores the way in which our inward being connects with the outer world. It is derived from a series of exercises created and tested by Adam McLean, a scholar of the hermetic tradition, as an introduction to the development of the alchemical imagination.[4] It is an excellent exercise for uniting soul and sensing.

The exercise involves becoming aware of the soul dimension of your sense experience. Think of it as a way of focusing on the border between the sense realm and the soul realm. Begin by consciously following a slight sound. You might, for example, ring a small bell or strike a chime. Do not just listen to the sound, but feel your consciousness ray out toward the sound and then return inward. At first, you may feel that it is only the sound that comes to meet your ear, and you may not be able to experience your hearing extending into the world. If you're unable to sense the latter, it indicates a degree of numbing of the body. You may have to practice this phase of the exercise for a while until you feel a tangible quality of following your consciousness out to the source of the sound and letting it return to your body.

Try the same experiment with sight. Look at an object in the room, across the way from where you are sitting. Follow your consciousness out to the object you are looking at, and then let it return to your body. Try to feel the subtle quality of your vision going out to meet the object and returning. Then, do the same exercise with touch. Feel your consciousness going out through the hand to the object you are touching and returning to your body. Then do the exercise with movement. Move your arm to grasp something, and while doing so feel the subtle way in which the object also makes itself available for your grasp. You can also do a similar exercise with balance. Go to the edge of a high place protected by a fence or railing. Notice the dizziness, and how imbalance invites fear. In a few moments, however, the dizziness diminishes and fear is banished. More is going on than becoming accustomed to the precarious place. Your soul-body has actually moved to fill the whole of the abyss, and you are now supported by the soul qualities of the world.

In each of these sense modalities, you will begin to feel an awareness of the relationship between your inner being and your perception. It is the relationship that is important, a clear sensing of a movement, a current going from your inner life, through the sense, out to the object, and then returning. Now, begin to focus on the awareness of the relationship itself, and begin to form inwardly a picture of this awareness as a clear glass flask. This image pictures the subtle border between soul and sensing. Once the image has been formed, stabilize it so that it remains a conscious image for a few minutes.

As the exercise continues, you will find images, thoughts, and feelings arising quite naturally. Do not try to avoid them, but let them develop and then watch them dissolve. These images arise out of the unconscious. See the images dissolve and come to rest at the bottom of the container as a deep interior darkness. See the glass container with the inner eye, and at the same time the deep interior darkness at the bottom of the container. After a few minutes, erase the image from consciousness and stay in the emptiness as long as possible.

An important cognitive element characterizes these exercises. One should not just go through the exercises and expect them to have an effect; one ought to be conscious of the kind of attention present while doing them. The bodily feelings are not the emphasis in these meditations. Once you become aware of that quality of consciousness, it is unmistakable. A subtle inner joy arises and spreads through the body. You feel as if you can breathe deeply again, and realize that you had not even noticed that this ability had diminished, perhaps a long time ago. You realize that you have been in a state of fear and did not even know it. A quality of spontaneity is present, as if you now feel ready to follow the promptings of the soul, which have been frozen for a long time.

This kind of sensory work certainly does not stop us from encountering fear and being affected by it. It can prevent fear from having its way, from taking over, but it is a work that now has to become more or less regular, and conscious. And in truth, this work is but a first, small step, one of many changes we must make to counter the presence of fear. Such work, while it must be conscious, can become a habit, something done regularly, and not just after encountering a particular and strong instance of fear.

CHAPTER 3

Terrorism, Time Collapse, and Anger: New Appearances of Fear in the World

A liveliness of the senses is essential to maintaining the soul. The life of imagination can then radiate into the world. Awakening the sensitivity of the body, however, also makes us more sensitive to the presence of differentiating patterns of fear that we must contend with. We do not create these patterns but rather find ourselves engaged with what depth psychology would call archetypal regions, each of which must be worked with in different ways. Meeting these patterns and responding to them in healthy ways requires developing a clear imagination of the many discreet regions of fear.

Until you imagine something thoroughly, you cannot participate in it thoroughly. If we approach fear by hoping to stop it through external means alone, we are bringing the wrong tools to bear. The real power of fear resides in our wish to avoid it, and the result of such repression is that it then takes us over completely.

The first capacity we need to develop is a deeply felt realization that this destroyer is also the great awakener. We will get nowhere if we do not begin by valuing our fears; this is not to say we need to invite them in, but to understand that they are already here, all around us, some affecting us more, some less. The threshold at the edge of security and comfort is crossed when we accept fear as a real presence, and not just as a subjective response to what we may perceive as a threat to our well-being. And once that threshold has been crossed, we have to follow through and find healthy ways of working to balance the presence of fear within us.

Suppose, for example, a child wakes up in the middle of the night crying loudly. When the mother gets up and comes to her, the child says that there is something in the closet—a purple man, grinning, about to grab her. If the mother tells the child that there is really nothing there, that it was just a bad dream, fear has then found a foothold and will continue to get stronger. But, if the mother comes into the room, goes to the closet, opens the door, takes a broom and sweeps out the creature, would not the child's fear be diminished? When we accept fear as a reality—even as a reality of the imagination—

it becomes something more than just a subjective response, and we can begin to work out healthy ways of countering it. The child, in the second instance, is not left thinking that nothing can be done, or that fear is not real. The fear has been valued, and dealt with. The things in the world that seem to cause fear, I suggest, are, from the viewpoint of the soul, not causes but manifestations of fear—fear showing itself in the world.

The soul, in its deepest regions, does not distinguish between what is real and what is subjective. It cannot be taught to do so. Our conscious minds have to respect the laws of the soul's nature, how it functions, and how to work with its reality on its own terms. Let us now look, from the soul's point of view, at some of the new realities of fear that we encounter in our daily life. These fears may seem so large that we have difficulty understanding what we as individuals can do about them. We may not be able to work directly on war, crime, environmental pollution, or disease, but we can work on how our soul is engaged with such fearful matters. The soul is engaged with these matters and has impressions of them that live within us; I intend to show that a new line of soul work can bring about actual change in us and in the world.

Terrorism

We confront now, almost daily, reports of terrorist attacks throughout the world. Within the past few years we have seen commercial airplanes bombed, poison gas released into a major subway, a federal building bombed, another bomb exploded in the parking garage of a major skyscraper, a railroad train sent hurling off a bridge, and bomb packages sent through the mail. At first, it seemed that terrorism could be attributed to enemies without, to radical groups in foreign countries; we were shocked to find that our next-door neighbors can also be perpetrators. With terrorism, fear becomes amplified a thousandfold. Fear becomes a commodity bought and sold, exported and imported, transported anywhere; it becomes a tangible thing, respecting no boundaries. It may be just around the corner for any of us, ready to leap out without any warning whatsoever.

The measures taken to defend against this form of fear also contribute to the dehumanizing process. We are subjected to guards at the airport, the courthouse, schools, sports events. Video cameras watch us at the bank, the store, the parking lot. There to protect us, they nevertheless turn us into objects and cause a contraction of the soul. They make us all more mean-spirited, paranoid, mistrustful.

Terror on this scale turns fear into a god—invisible, all-powerful, a great and mighty punisher, the lord of death himself. To wield death in such a manner, the terrorist joins his very being with death. He is no longer afraid of death and could just as well convey the bomb to its appointed site on his person as through any other means. His life means nothing to him, and thus neither does anyone else's.

We live our lives as usual, go to work, go home, yet with a new constant awareness; in the next moment we may die. Life is in great part a preparation for death. But terrorism, besides bringing death into conscious imagination, brings images of being disfigured, paralyzed, maimed, or perhaps imprisoned, tortured. Terrorism kills the sense that we have a future, a life destiny. Once the possibility of being subjected to this sort of terror enters the soul life, our capacity to look toward the future with joy and anticipation dulls. Our interest subtly withdraws from the world; there seems to be nothing of value to do anymore unless it is for our own immediate benefit or pleasure. The effect of terrorism is not merely to kill people but to commit soul murder on those of us not directly affected. It views people as objects, and we become objects, even to ourselves.

Terror cannot tolerate ambiguity, metaphor, imagination, creativity. Terrorism literalizes death, robbing us of the capacity to imagine death as a natural culmination of our time here on earth.[1] Such an imagination requires us to see life as an ongoing counterpart to death. Our natural inclination is always to feel and imagine life as a conflict with death, and we live in the faith that the force of life is always the stronger. Terror reverses this, making death stronger, more prominent, more in control. The terrorist no longer holds an imagination of life as having any force. The potential for each of us to become our own terrorist can be found in the loss of faith in life. We throw up our arms in disgust when we hear of another incident of terror, not knowing what can be done to stop it. We grow accustomed to seeing bombed buildings burning, people running and screaming, blood, and lifeless bodies. In the presence of such images, it becomes difficult to retain hope in humanity.

The presence of terror in the world is like a great process of compression. Living in the midst of such images of death eats away at the most ordinary forms of human connection, producing numbness and isolation. For example, we are asked to be more on guard, to be aware of anyone leaving an unattended bag or parcel. A twinge of worry enters anyone who travels on a train, plane, bus, subway. The news now announces terrorism alerts. We have been told to expect many more incidents of international terrorism, with the United States a prime target. I know of families who are afraid to travel together on the same plane.

This form of fear seems to defy the basic formulation that was made at the very beginning of this work—that becoming free of fear does not mean getting rid of it but rather developing the inner capacities to stay with it, which gradually produces a transformation, not only within us but also within the world. Of course it seems that the best solution is to find a direct way to eliminate terrorism. We always want to do away with what we do not like. But as with any fear, it would be a mistake to assume that eliminating the proximate cause would bring an end to the fear altogether. Getting rid of terrorism without changing the undercurrent of hatred associated with it can only mean exchanging it for some other fearful situation—like a removal of human freedom or living in some sort of police state. When we assume that a threat can be removed without inner change, we do not see the phenomenon for what it is.

Instead of asking how to eliminate this atrocious thing, our question might be, What is this fear doing in the world at this time? How can we conceive of it, and see its characteristics clearly, so that it no longer dominates us? This reality has a will of its own, which is greater and mightier than any individual will. The terrorist is someone who has given over his personal will completely to something far more encompassing.

One characteristic of this impersonal will is that it is nameless. Terrorists seldom make themselves known, and when they do, it is typically in the name of a group. Even when a particular terrorist is caught, the personality of the individual involved is usually of no consequence. Generally, the identity of the victims does not matter to the terrorist either—it can be ordinary people going to work, a subway full of commuters, a commercial airliner. Even the Unabomber, although he sent his packages to particular individuals, was attacking primarily what he saw as the facelessness of modern technology. Bombs are secondary to the weaponry of chaos and anonymity.

Anonymity breeds violence. You can see it bubbling up in the defacing of walls, or surging beneath the surface in schools where individuality so easily gets lost. The cities we construct in the name of civilization consist of faceless buildings, repetitive shopping malls, chain stores that are exactly the same all around the country.

Because we live in mass anonymity, we are already immersed in terror, and the actual act only makes visible in a violent way what we are already living. When such incidents occur, we feel shock, horror, and disgust, but we do not connect these feelings to the ongoing conditions of our lives.

For example, a person in one of our workshops had this to say concerning an event of terrorism:

The terrorist bombing of the city bus in Israel evoked an emotional response. I saw pictures of the bombing on television, and I recall being overwhelmed with shock and the physical feeling of being hit in the gut and losing my breath. The senselessness of it all, the waste of lives, the unfairness, wrongness, craziness of the world screamed at me, and I remember leaving the room and going outside to walk. I walked for about thirty minutes, and by the time I returned home the event was more or less gone from my consciousness.

Another person in a workshop says:

There's so many of these events you lose track and they all seem the same. The same dull pain with each. What can you do? You just hold on, you don't let it get to you, laugh it off even. The odds are so remote it will happen to you, and the world is just feeling lousier these days, what else is new?

These kinds of responses are quite understandable. Not many people are able to live with the ongoing feeling of terror. Here is an example of a person who experiences more vividly the reality of terror:

On hearing this news of the terrorist bombing, my body went into shock. This for me is a state of paralysis. I may be going about daily life, but inside my chest area, behind my sternum, into my lungs and heart, a stiffening has occurred. At first I felt a complete standstill as if everything had stopped functioning; it is as if I have to remind myself to breathe, to swallow, as if a hole has developed in this part of me. I cannot allow myself to feel, it is too dangerous. When I do allow myself to feel, I feel the unbelievable anguish a parent feels when a child dies. I go back and forth in feeling rage toward the killer and fear.

These responses to the presence of terrorism show how the facelessness of our world has become a place in which to hide oneself in order to avoid the terrible pain that would result from letting someone else's suffering affect us deeply. Little do we realize, however, that by hiding in the anonymity of the world we are adding to the facelessness that feeds the nihilistic imagination of terrorism. And it's exactly this sort of repression that gives fear its best opportunity to infiltrate the soul.

Placing the problem of terrorism at the very center of modern civilization seems overwhelming. What can an individual do in the face of a global difficulty? Individually, we may be able to do very little to stop terrorism. Each of us can, however, work with how the soul is engaged with the terror it produces. The numbing that occurs with the tandem realities of terror and anonymity is a soul condition, a kind of splitting off of soul life from bodily life. The result of this kind of splitting is shown in the examples above. Our feeling grows dull, cynicism reigns, and our intellect works to convince us that real terror cannot happen to us. The real work to be done here concerns consciously keeping soul engaged with body, and is different from what was presented in the last chapter, where the central concern was countering the anesthesia of the senses. In the case of terror, we have to do a different kind of soul work.

Body and soul are more like two sides of a leaf than like two discrete entities. The body is the soul's expression in the world, and if the body becomes dulled the soul has limited means of engaging the world. Very subtle matters are addressed here. How do you tell if your soul life has become more or less detached from bodily life? The degree of rigidity in our attitudes provides an indication. Am I intolerant? Do I have dogmatic, inflexible ideas? Am I prone to fanaticism? Do I oppose necessary change? Do I feel it necessary to conform to the power of authority?

To the degree that one finds such characteristics in oneself, an important correlation typically follows: it is likely that one will also find rigidity in one's body posture. The way to bring flexibility back to the soul and the body is through the path of imagination. Developing a conscious imagining of the subtle activity of the body re-engages the soul with the body. For example, Bernard Lievegoed, a Dutch organizational consultant, has proposed a series of imaginative exercises that focus on the processes of the body.[2] The intention is to develop the capacity to experience our body as a living activity rather than as a static entity or as an assemblage of it as physiological operations. The imaginative exercises, done in a regular way, actually awaken us to the presence of fear, without overwhelming us. One exercise is described below:

Each day for about five minutes, you should free yourself from thoughts, activities, and concerns. Close your eyes and do the following:

1. First focus on the inner image of your physical being. Feel the force of gravity working in the weight of your limbs. Remember a time when you were ill, or when you came home after a long hike—any occasion when you felt the heaviness of your body. Reflect on the crystallizing processes of the body; remember growing up, how flexible your body once was, and how it has gradually become more stiff.

2. Direct your attention to the fluid processes of the body. Picture the force of the blood pulsing from the heart, flowing outward, slowing down in channels, almost coming to a standstill in the capillaries. Picture your blood collecting again in slow streams, which, with greater and greater speed return to the heart, disappearing in a

whirlpool into the right chamber of the heart. Picture the initial surge, as well as the standstill in the vortex when reentering the heart.

Picture the fluids flowing into the stomach and large intestine and being reabsorbed by the large intestine. This motion is like the ebb and flow of the tide on a beach. Picture the lymph slowly flowing through the body, around the cells, quietly merging into the bloodstream. Picture the cerebral fluid bubbling up into the cerebral cavity, bathing the brain and the spinal cord, and then being reabsorbed again down in the spinal column.

3. Picture air entering the lungs, dividing into thousands of air sacs, where the movement comes to a rest. Then picture the air mixing with the blood and being carried throughout the body, giving new life. Then picture breathing out carbon dioxide, collected from all over the body. Picture the carbon dioxide returning to the air, being taken up by plants and trees, which release oxygen.

4. Feel the inner warmth of the body. The highest temperature occurs in the digestive organs, while the coolest parts of the body are the skin and extremities. Picture warmth radiating from your body. Picture a state of enthusiasm, and imagine how this state converts into bodily warmth, and how this warmth lightens the body and overcomes fatigue.

This imagination of our body should be conceived of

as the elemental body—our body of Earth, Water, Air, and Fire. Developing this imagination places us in connection with the elemental beings of the world. More important, this practice develops the sense of intercorporeality: how we are in intimate relation with other people, and even with the cosmos. The soul breathes from the deepest point within and then out to the widest expanses of the world.

Here are several brief descriptions of how the above exercise affected some workshop participants:

> I was pouring water into a bucket a few days after practicing this exercise and found myself transfixed by the water in a surprising way. I just had to stand there and look at it for a while. Also, walking by a river, I felt the water as an extension of my body.

> I noticed things around me in a quite different way. I looked at the furniture and inanimate objects with a great sense of interest at how they were made and the quality of the wood or stone. Colors and plant life were also very radiant for a period of time after the exercise.

> Imagining the elemental qualities of the body filled me with a weaving feeling of love moving through my body. I felt reverence for my body and was filled with gratitude. I felt a sense of awe just looking at others.

Paying attention to our body hardly seems to be a way to stop terrorism. Remember, though, that the concerns here are how the soul responds to the presence of terrorism in the world and how to assure the health of the soul-body. Such concerns are not self-centered. Rather, they are oriented toward working against the dehumanizing effects of terrorism, which are far more threatening than the deaths such acts bring about. Terrorism will be a much less effective force if we do not allow ourselves to become infected with fear.

The Acceleration of Time

If I am in a large city such as New York, and walk into Central Park, time changes. It has more duration, a slower tempo. When I walk out of the park, time changes again, accelerating on the busy street. The change in our feeling of time — that time is now speeding up — results from an imbalance between duration and tempo.[3] Duration decreases, while tempo increases. Not only has tempo increased, but it has changed in character as well. Rhythm has an organic tempo. But, when, for example, we spend each workday in the city with constant automobile traffic, the rhythm of our walk begins to subtly imitate the tempo of the mechanized things around us.

A mountain may seem timeless, but things of the world

have their own duration as well. There is the duration of the day; the duration of a plant that has flowered; the duration of each season. We bring tempo to the picture. We pick up the pace, become hurried, have too many things to do, try to squeeze as much as we can into a day. The organic tempo that belongs to us, which balances us with the world, has been altered from the rhythm of the heartbeat to the mechanical pace of the machine and the fitful rhythm of the electronic world. With the ubiquity of computers, faxes, Internet, cellular phones, e-mail, and global communications, the tempo of modern life has been accelerated beyond recognition.

What have such changes done to the soul? The soul requires duration of time—rich, thick, deep, velvety time—and it thrives on rhythm. Soul can't be hurried or harried. It has to take in events slowly, ruminating over them, turning them into its own experiences. When the soul is instead bombarded with a rapid sequence of events that have little depth, another kind of fear enters soul life. We experience this fear as "time is running out." This colloquialism expresses a soul reality. It is as if the time soul lives in is a fluid, and it is being squeezed. For the soul to be deprived of duration and tempo takes away its capacity for expression in the world. We live in temporal anxiety, as if we are about to come to some unknown abrupt end.

The acceleration we experience with the modern world is something quite different from the normal expansions and contractions of time that occur when we live more according to the natural rhythm of the day. Ordinarily, if I am doing something I love, time goes by quickly, whereas if I am bored, it seems to crawl. When I am doing something that I love, I have joined myself, my own tempo, with what I am doing, and times seems to move more quickly. When I am not doing what I love, time seems to go on interminably. This natural relation to duration and tempo is often turned upside down by the pace of life today. Now, if I am doing something that I do not love, time doesn't slow down at all. There is only more to do, more quickly: all tempo and no duration. Duration is actually present, but filled with dread rather than love. We dare not experience the dread—it may mean the loss of our job, or having to face that our work does not reflect what we want to be doing with our life. We come to live on the surface of time, and things lose their depth. We may go through many events in the day and experience nothing because the soul has not had the opportunity to roll the events over, to feel them from many different points of view, to review them, hear their particular tonal qualities, mull over what comes in, breathe in and out with an event, extracting its essence and life importance. At its core, the fear inspired by the speeding up of time, seen from the soul's perspective, is that the soul will not develop through its engagement with the world. It fears being left out of life.

There are aspects of modern life apart from the "electrification" of time that diminish our experience of duration. Drugs such as speed, or cocaine, or crack affect the experience of time radically. Cocaine and crack increase the rate of metabolism. When metabolism is high, time is actually experienced as slowing down. Children have higher metabolism than older people, and their sense of time has more duration. Older people, whose metabolism has slowed down, experience time as moving much faster. Seen in this way, those who take crack and cocaine are trying to counter the effects of a world that is speeding up. These drugs also affect the nervous system, however, so the results are very mixed. Taking speed, on the other hand—a completely unnatural substance that works more on the nervous system than on the metabolism and produces a speeding up of time—can be seen as an attempt to solve the situation by trying to outrun it.[4]

A third aspect of fear produced by the acceleration of time is the phenomenon of callousness. Cold, hard, and swift, callousness leads us to judge people without taking time to understand their situation. When corporations downsize, hundreds, even thousands of people lose their jobs instantly, just so that the reduction of costs shows up as an increase in profits. No time is taken for long-range solutions. The intent here is not to blame corporations for the change in our relation with time but to describe how this change shows up in the world. Here are some observations made by a workshop participant who works in a large corporation:

> The senior managers in my division rarely last longer than two years. As a result, things are constantly in turmoil with a big part of my life being dedicated to educating upper management about what it is that we do. We spend as much time teaching the people who have come in to "clean things up" as we do thinking about the future.
>
> Our products have always been known for their quality, but the bigger we get the more the quality of our product suffers. This is very difficult, for the people here take great pride in their work. All we hear is "faster and cheaper" with the expectation that the quality won't erode.
>
> New initiatives and announcements of all kinds come down from the top all the time, and the majority of the time they dissipate in a few days. Those who take these initiatives seriously tend to get themselves all worked up to the point where they do damage only to find out a few days later that the initiative is actually a dead issue. The manager must be able to absorb blows and give out calmness and reflective responses. The ability to wait is very important.[5]

When heart is removed from our actions, time manifests as callousness. Not only callousness to others, but cruelty to Earth—to her creatures, to her trees and plants and animals—characterize the world caught in the frenzy of speed. It is quicker to devastate a forest than to build within it; it is quicker to tear down buildings than to carefully restore them; it is quicker to dump chemicals into the nearest river or waste dump than to spend the time and money to reprocess them for good use.

The cruelty of time that is all pace and repetition with little duration also shows up in our personal lives. We don't have time to really listen; in the middle of a telephone conversation, we put our friend on call-waiting. We become impatient as our children tell us the events of their day at school. We have almost no time alone, no sense of a place of sanctuary within the home. The only regular experience of anything resembling duration comes from television. Here we live in a kind of monotony of duration, for instead of leaving us feeling renewed and refreshed it leaves us feeling emptied and tired.

We can find balance to temporal anxiety and the dread that comes from time having no spaciousness by taking up, and regularly practicing, some form of meditation. Anyone who has practiced meditation becomes aware of the remarkable flexibility of time experience. For example, when meditation goes well, a half-hour seems like seconds; when it does not go so well, a few minutes is experienced as hours. Meditation that can deepen our experiences of time and be taken over into daily life requires only about five to ten minutes of clock-time a day. Longer meditations can gradually pull us away from the world, as we may begin to find the spiritual and cosmic worlds more alluring and appealing than the earthly one.

During each meditation session you should aim to fill your consciousness with only one idea. Or it can equally be an image. The idea should be of an ordinary object, one with which we have no particular connection, such as a paper clip. You then circle the idea with all the qualities belonging to that object—it is metal, oblong-shaped, holds papers together, and so on. At first, it is likely that you will think on the object with words. With practice, it is possible to perceive without words. After more practice, it is as if the object thinks itself, though you should never let it go on like a fantasy; maintain clear consciousness. After doing this meditation for a few minutes, the next step is to completely extinguish concentrating on the idea. Then try to remain in a complete void as long as possible.

If you choose to meditate an image rather than an idea, then the task is simply to make an inner image of an object that you observe. Don't just remember something that you have seen, but find something—a rock, a pencil, a simple plant, and observe it for a few moments. Then make an inner image of that object. Don't elaborate or embellish the image, but make an inner image of the object that is exactly like the outer perception. Stabilize the image and then hold it for a few minutes. As with the idea, after holding the image extinguish it and remain in the void.

Such meditation helps one regain the experience of duration. In meditation on the object, at first our thoughts go from one aspect of the object to another, and with the image we focus from one aspect of the image to another. With sustained practice, it begins to feel like the whole idea or image is there all at once. We do not enter into timelessness, but rather into duration. We gradually become able to hold all aspects of the object or the image together at once rather than moving from one character- istic to another. Such an experience of duration is differ- ent from, say, walking in the hills and experiencing a majestic mountain. In nature, we are placed in a situation where duration rules and we simply enjoy it. With this exercise we are working to make duration conscious. We are developing a capacity of the soul.[6]

The meditation should be short in order not to inter- fere with the duties and responsibilities of our lives. This practice does not lead to dramatic results; the effects move subtly over into daily life, and the experience of duration is renewed, according to where we are and what we are doing. The important part of the exercise consists of developing the will to do it. To concentrate on a single thing for a few minutes without anything else being allowed to intrude requires a force of the will. Having done that, extinguishing the idea or image is a second act of will that must be as strong as that which generated the idea or image in the first place.

Another thing to notice in doing this practice is your breathing. At first, the idea or image that one focuses on can be sustained only by coordinating the rhythm of breathing with the process of meditation. Gradually, the aim should be the ability to concentrate independently of the breath. Our body participates in the time realm of duration as well as tempo. The breath is connected with tempo, while for this exercise we are trying to discover the experience of duration.

A further aspect of this form of meditation is that doing the exercise daily does not make it easier. Indeed, it becomes somewhat more difficult. It can become more automatic, yet when this happens it is no longer meditating but merely thinking about the exercise in the past. Each time the exercise is done, it is an act of creation. When a true artist paints one picture, the next picture does not become easier, but rather more difficult—that is, if the artist is truly engaged in the creative process and not just in painting pictures. Meditation is also an art. We call it a practice because one never masters it. I know people who have done this little practice daily for more than twenty years.

Violence

We are familiar with the many large expressions of overwhelming passion: war; nationalism; drive-by shootings; gang violence; the actions of disgruntled employees going armed to their places of work; abuse of children, wives, and the elderly; shootings in schools. This anger works on the souls of everyone, and we all have a harder time containing anger that seems to have no source but comes up now and then, taking us off guard.

Here are some descriptions of anger from workshop participants, very much like experiences that we all, under certain conditions, discover within us and that can be very frightening:

Just the other day at work, I felt a sudden twinge of strong anger at my friend Charles. I told him that I really liked a certain film I saw and he quickly "corrected" me, as he often does. It sounds like a small thing, but his tone was angry and his demeanor condescending. The anger ignited in my stomach, first hot and then quickly changed to a cold sensation. Like a chain reaction, my stomach went cold, causing my heart to pound rapidly and my consciousness to dim. He commented on my anger, grinning. I felt pure rage welling up inside of me. It took me quite a while to recover.

I had this amazing urge to kick my cat the other day. Even though I consider him to be neck-and-neck with the Dalai Lama in holiness, I thought, Who would know? He's old and grouchy and his yowling had been getting on my nerves. Here I was, late for work, rushing around, and the cat is yowling his head off at me. It was as if my leg had a mind of its own. It was going to move and there wasn't much I could do about it. I remember this all so well because there was no way I was going to harm my cat. I had to sit down and get calm.

Both my children were in the kitchen with me. I had asked them to stop fighting with each other, but they continued. I felt, all of a sudden, that I was getting hot, the temperature in me was rising. I stopped breathing regularly. I felt both hot and a rising coldness through the middle of my body from the waist up to my throat. It is all accumulating there. My head was hot, my heart was cold. The noise, the fighting, the talking back all join together. My heart beat faster and faster, a sound like a growl starts and then fills me and I roar like a bear. As this is happening I am in my body and watching at the

same time. It was amazing. At that moment I knew I had
to walk away and let this pass.[7]

Our understanding of the human soul has not kept
pace with other kinds of understanding, and this has
resulted in a radical imbalance. In this particular realm of
emotion and passion, we both decry and feel attracted to
being overwhelmed. We feel the need to get ever closer
to passion lest it be lost altogether, but since we do not
know how to approach it, passion can take over completely. An invisible line is crossed, and we are sent into
the raging heat of the unformed soul.

Even as violent passions spill forth from the trenches of
foreign countries, on the screen, in the back alleys of the
city, behind the closed doors of the house next door, we
are all being infected with fear. Hyper-arousal is one way
this fear expresses itself. Can you walk on a dark street at
night without being startled by the least noise? Don't we
often feel irritable, more edgy, and not sure where these
feelings are coming from? We feel ongoing apprehensive-
ness, a fearfulness without an object. Many people find it
increasingly difficult to sleep, an indication of unease, of
fright. Our body is always on the alert for danger.

Another expression of living in the midst of a world in
which passion has gone wild is a diminishing of memory.
Memory becomes more picture-oriented, more iconic,

less verbal, more like that of a child. This mode of remembering lacks detail, nuance, context, and is more concrete and literalistic. Imagination also suffers; it too becomes literal, having pictures in one's mind rather than the capacity to make images that are complex and subtle, that involve all the sense modalities, not just visualization alone.

Behavior is also affected; it becomes repetitive, uncreative, almost as if one is in a trance. We drive to work and don't remember most of the trip. We put keys into a briefcase and a few minutes later we search the house frantically for them. We seem to be on automatic pilot. But when nearly everyone is in a trance, such behavior appears normal. Violence, or constant presentations of it in the media, brings about a general dimming of consciousness in us all, providing an opening for what will later be described as the double, a force of a quite real nature, beyond anything of a personal psychological nature.

These symptoms are very similar to what someone who has experienced actual trauma undergoes. For the rest of us, they are also present, though not as obvious or dramatic. A narrowing of consciousness nonetheless characterizes our time: numbness on the one hand, and rage right beneath the surface on the other. People go through the motions of living, but it is life lived at a distance, observing the life one lives rather than being in it. But since all looks normal, these constrictive symptoms go unrecognized. At any moment, uncontrollable anger may erupt.

The flaming up of passions spreads through the world like an epidemic disease that varies in intensity from place to place. It is definitely becoming more pervasive. This evening as I write, the news is reporting that three local teenage boys made a bomb and intended to blow up their school. The boys learned how to build the bomb on the Internet. Later the same evening another program ran a report on the growing phenomenon of "road rage." One man's spouse had been killed, shot by an individual in a passing car who became angry over the way the first man was driving. Last year, more than fifteen hundred deaths resulted from angered drivers attacking other drivers.

The word *passion* covers a great deal of psychic terrain. Anger is an emotion, but as it modulates into rage, it takes on qualities of a passion. We are not able to control our passions to the degree we do our emotions. But there is also passionate love, passionate thought, passionate action. Is passion just emotion intensified? Something additional seems to be involved. What factor accounts for why, when emotion rises to a certain intensity, we no longer merely have that emotion but become it? The emotion becomes autonomous; it becomes larger than our capacity to control it. The flaming of passion in human beings reflects the climatic conditions of the world, the gathering storm clouds of hatred spreading across every continent. Anyone may be infected at any time by this collective force. The individual who shot the woman in the car next to him on the expressway pumped sixteen shots into the car. He later said that he had absolutely no memory of the event. He remembered the circumstances, that he was being tailgated by the car, and that the driver of the other car taunted him. He remembered taking the gun out of his glove compartment, but he had no memory of firing it. This man had never done anything remotely similar in his life. Hatred does not have to seethe in the breast of an individual. Suddenly, without warning, it comes, and it takes over. Or it may seethe for years or, for a nation, for centuries. It may start out as a prank, looking for a thrill, as with the children making the bomb to blow up the school. Hatred can be completely unpredictable, and it can leave just as quickly as it came. This force inspires fear in us all.

The above descriptions of people going through upsurges of anger reveal an important aspect of soul life. The experience of anger as felt in the body is depicted as hot and icy cold, simultaneously. It is the icy cold aspect of anger that we most fear in others—and in ourselves.

There are two kinds of fire in the soul—the warm fire of love and the icy fire of hatred. If the fire of love does not burn, then the fire of hatred becomes all-consuming. Picture a candle flame; it is like the fire of love, but it needs the wick to transform the substance of the wax into its flame; the substance of the wax is like all that is within us that remains unknown, in the dark. If the wax itself starts to burn, it spreads quickly and uncontrollably. The fire itself is the same in both cases, but in one instance it creates light and in another burns up the house. Hatred inverts love. It is like wax catching fire—an inversion of love, the negative of love. Hatred devours while love radiates. The flaming of passion is more like an implosion than an explosion, excessive contraction of the soul rather than expansion. The presence of the fear in the world inspired by the flaming of passions can make us aware of the need for purification of soul as a balance to this destructive force.

How does one work toward purity of soul? The very notion has all but disappeared, though every mystic and spiritual seeker knows well that it is a necessary work. The notion became too filled with negative connotations, and it seemed to disparage everything that was enjoyable. Then the notion was codified into rules and regulations, and instead of purification, repression resulted. The primary inner work of soul purification, though, does not involve suppressing or repressing anything. The primary work is watchfulness, the self-observation of one's soul life. We cannot peer directly at our soul, but we can watch its expressions, both inner and outer.

What we now need to be watchful of is our images. Taking in all the pictures of violence, reading the stories of its outbreaks throughout the world, hearing the reports of murder and destruction—this greatly affects the soul, and affects it right at the border between soul and body. The terrible atrocities we see in the news sink right down to the level of the body. We experience a fearfulness in the body and live as if we have been traumatized, even if we're unable to locate traumatic events that have actually happened to us. We may be surprised at the anger we seem to carry and how easy it is to be on the edge of exploding for little reason.

The first step toward purification of the soul is developing the ability to be fully present to the force of anger, even hatred, within ourselves without directing this force at anyone, including ourselves. When you are able to be present to the stirrings of deep anger, they will give rise to images. The images may be of a violent nature, such as an image of doing something hurtful to the one who seemed to provoke your fury. When such an image presents itself, what is most important is to refrain from acting out the image. Nor is there a need to go tell that person of the anger you feel, for in actual fact, he or she is most likely not responsible for your anger. The next step is to watch those images in order to hold an inner perception of them that is usually quickly obliterated—that they are all accompanied by deep fear.

Soul purification involves being able to live with the heat of emotions without repressing uncomfortable feelings or acting them out toward others. Purification is a kind of burning process, an inner heat, where the source of the heat, the means of the purification, is the poison itself. This notion that the healing is found with the poison is expressed in *The Zen Teachings of Bodhidharma*:

> The three realms are greed, anger, and delusion. To leave the three realms means to go from greed, anger, and delusion back to morality, meditation, and wisdom. Greed, anger, and delusion have no nature of their own. They depend on mortals. And anyone capable of reflection is bound to see that the nature of greed, anger, and delusion is the buddha-nature. Beyond greed, anger, and delusion there is no other buddha-nature. The sutras say, "Buddhas have only become buddhas while living with the three poisons and nourishing themselves on the pure Dharma." The three poisons are greed, anger, and delusion. [8]

All the anger in the world, responded to by the soul, becomes poison in the soul that, if acted out, creates more and more fear in the world. If the poison in the soul can be felt as a purifying heat within the soul—which occurs by becoming aware of our anger, and the fear within our anger—and holding it without acting it out, then this poison heals.

CHAPTER 4

*Perennial Fears with a New
Sting: Money, Relationships,
Suffering, and Death*

When we become frightened, a large part of our trepidation comes from expecting some unknown event to occur in the future, even if it's the very next moment. This expectation does not reside in thinking something is about to happen, for in such states of fear we may not be thinking clearly or at all. We experience the expectation directly in the body. When we are in the midst of something quite terrible, the bodily apprehension of what may come next is what sustains the terror. Terror allows no imagination of possibilities other than increased intensity of the panic.

Fears diminish soul life by eliminating a future of open possibilities. The kinds of image exercises suggested thus far are oriented toward restoring the capacity to imagine a future. What characterizes each of these exercises is the conscious act of creating images; and it can be further said that in doing so we are bringing about balance by creating alternate possibilities to the fears that have invaded every sector of the world.

This path to creating a future of open possibilities differs considerably from practices that ask us to turn away from what is difficult and to imagine the world as wonderful and rosy, affirming the goodness of the universe. Instead, I advocate clear understanding of the nature of fears, accompanied by image-making exercises that do not pretend such fear does not exist. These image-making exercises assure us that fears do not shut down our interior life, and they require and develop active, conscious effort.

Many of the fears that now plague us relate to a rapid change of the context of our lives. Three such contexts undergoing drastic change are the meaning of money and the economy, the assumptions concerning relationships of every sort, and the meaning of suffering and death. Enormous fears now cluster around the soul's engagement with these domains of experience.

Money Fears

Betty S. Flowers, an author and social theorist, has written on the mythic themes of America and how these themes are in the midst of drastic revision.[1] She puts forth the view that three myths have guided America until recent times. By "myth," she means the contexts of imagination that people live within, the concepts that give meaning to our existence and form the patterns of our actions in the world.

The first myth she identifies is the heroic myth of rugged individualism, of coming from humble origins, making it on one's own, facing the unknown, making sacrifices, gradually rising to prominence, and then giving something back to the community. This myth came to an end with the Vietnam War, for when the heroic warriors returned from battle there was no recognition and no welcoming to tell these people that their suffering and sacrifices were deeply significant to the whole community. There was an attempt to revive this myth with Desert Storm, but Americans did not quite believe it, as there was also a strong economic motive behind the Gulf War.

The second myth that Flowers says once brought us together as a community is of America as the "promised land," "the light unto nations." Hardly anyone in public leadership (except perhaps the Christian Coalition) dares to use the language of this myth anymore, fearing to offend the wide-ranging religious diversity of this nation. When President Clinton tried several years ago to rally Americans by speaking of making a "covenant" with the people, which is essentially a religious way of speaking, he was not heard. The Republicans, however, used a different metaphor, that of a "contract with America." This legalistic, businesslike metaphor had force, indicating another sort of change in our imagination.

The third story that no longer holds is the democratic myth. This myth says that everyone has an equal chance, that everyone has a voice, that there is liberty and justice for all. We are now painfully coming to recognize how one's socioeconomic status determines one's chances in life, and how justice depends on whether you have the money to hire expensive lawyers. Self-interest has replaced the common good.

The predominant myth within which we all now live is an economic myth. What we do, how we live, and what we value are largely determined by monetary worth. Money, no doubt, has always had enormous power, but now it overshadows all other values. The fears surrounding money have to do not only with survival but also with the loss of identity associated with not buying into this myth. The difficulty with the economic myth, as with all myths based on a divisive illusion, is that it leaves out the soul. Statistics, polls, gross national product, inflation rates, production growth, and measures of the global economy form the abstract fabric of this way of organizing the world. There is nothing for the soul to relate to, nothing in the outer world that reflects its own mode of reality, which arises through sacred images. The fear hiding behind all of the vacuous statistical rhetoric of the economic myth is the fear of living without a sacred view of the world. Economics, a word that means "care of the household," can be a sacred matter; it is not economics per se that constitutes fear, but the sort of economy that depends on the festishizing of material wealth. Still, we must ask, what gives these numbers such power?

The myth of modern economics cannot hold people together as a whole community, and the world begins fracturing into those who possess and those who are dispossessed. Separation always forms a basis of fears, and in the case of economics, this separation is between those who have socioeconomic power and status and those who do not.

Economic fear also has a great deal to do with how people are treated in the workplace. Corporate culture treats individuals as units. This attitude has infected nearly all of work, whether one happens to work for a corporation or not, and it relies on fear. Here is a description of layoffs in a large corporation:

> The way the layoffs were handled was legalistic, efficient, and demeaning. They hired two security guards to make sure things didn't get out of control. In the meetings where people were told they were being laid off, the vice president read from a prepared statement, the same statement for each employee. Next the employee

was escorted to his or her desk where they had little time
to pack up, and then they were escorted to the door. This
was all carried out in front of the rest of the company.[2]

This picture reveals the way in which fear has become an unavoidable part of corporate life. The layoffs
described were evidently orchestrated to make the rest
of the employees afraid. When corporations treat individuals in this way, soul has no place in daily endeavors.
Work is diminished to the banality of keeping the economic machine running efficiently. Our talents and abilities are called upon for a task, but these talents and
abilities are utilized to accomplish what someone else
wants in the world, usually higher profits. The creativeness of our spirit and the depths of our individual soul
often have to be relinquished, which results in working in
fear. Creativeness and individuality interfere with effi-
ciency and productivity, even though in the long run
these qualities contribute most to a lasting, viable business. These days, however, business looks toward short-
term gain as the way to perpetuate itself. Receiving a
salary is often the only compensation for forgetting who
we are. A first small step—something each of us can do
to assure that we do not sell our soul for work—is to perform an exercise daily, to build up the forces of the soul
in the context of work that does little to nourish it.

Exercise: Imagine a scene that is typical of your job. You may, for example, picture writing at a computer, or teaching a class, or preparing a legal document—whatever your job consists of on a daily basis. Then, when you have this inner picture and have stabilized it, dissolve the picture into a ball of light. Then let the light re-form into a figure, the figure of a man or a woman, say, or any other form, such as a troll, or an angel, or another sort of being. Then ask this being, "What is your work in the world?" Do not be concerned if you feel as if you are making up an answer out of your head. Just let it happen. What does this figure say to you? After your conversation is completed, thank this being, and let the figure again dissolve into a ball of light, and then let the light return to your own image of your job. Then open your eyes. Doing this exercise periodically may produce quite interesting results. For example, you may find that while your job may seem the same day in and day out, the soul and spirit dimensions of what you are doing may change frequently. Being present to such change will bring new life to your job. You may also discover that what you think you are doing is something quite different from what your soul and spirit are doing.

In the past, when economic fear based on class distinctions came to dominate the whole of a culture, the situation was ripe for violent revolution. The intention of an exercise such as this is to bring about an inner revolution, the goal of which is to preserve soul. The difficulty in being treated with brutal anonymity lies in the fact that one can become forgetful of being more than a mere function. But if, under the rather dire circumstances prescribed by the economic myth, we keep an inner liveliness of soul and spirit, the possibility of creating a genuine, embracing myth remains open. The many times I have done this exercise with groups of people has shown me that, indeed, a new myth is attempting to emerge, and that this myth has to do with being of selfless service to others. The reports from people who have done this exercise attest to this. One person, who works as a writer for a popular children's television series, imagined a scene of himself as sitting at his desk, writing scripts. When this task became an inner figure, he saw an angel who said that his work was to bring courage of heart into the world. This writer was amazed and a bit overwhelmed, and viewed what he had been doing for years in a completely new light. Another person considered her job as answering the telephone all day long. When this job became an inner figure, she saw a grandmotherly figure inviting people to dinner, and a group of people sitting around the table having a delicious dinner. When people do this exercise, they most often experience images having to do with service. The soul apparently feels most free from fear when it imagines doing something for others. The soul feels the call of the genuine needs of others.

While it might seem strange to approach such over-whelming economic fears by suggesting we exercise the imagination, the goal is not to solve the problem of money and its power in our culture. It is simply to pro-vide a way for the soul to keep from getting lost and for-gotten in the presence of fears surrounding money. If we can keep soul connected with our jobs, our re-imagined work life will go a long way to alleviate financial fears.

Fearful Relationships

Relationships of every sort today are filled with a great deal of apprehension. A teacher dare not touch a child, even in the most innocent manner, for fear of accusations of sexual abuse. One must be on guard at work, con-stantly vigilant of what one says in case it could be con-strued as harassment. An intimate relationship can turn into terrible, codependent battering. Marriages have less than a fifty-percent chance of lasting. Today's friend becomes tomorrow's bitter enemy. Husband turns against wife, child against parent, parent against child.

The illusion we live with is that relationships are always a safe haven. A relationship is felt to be a kind of vessel, a container in which we can be who we are without pretense, a place where we feel understood and cherished, no matter what others might think, a holy region where we can be strengthened to face the harshness of the wider world. If these qualities are not found in our relationships, something is thought to be wrong with the vessel. Therapies have been devised to make relationships into what we imagine they ought to be, ranging from talking through all feelings, to working at understanding the radical differences between men and women, to becoming aware of the inner image of the other person we carry. Few therapies, if any, focus on helping people see that relationships are terribly fraught, are becoming even more difficult, and to look at the wonder of why we engage in them at all.

Relationships carry their anxieties—the possibility of betrayal, disloyalty, abuse, indifference, neglect, hatred, anger, revenge, competition, degradation, abandonment. Yet we have high expectations of our special bonds with others—indeed, far too high. We rely on these bonds for our feelings of self-worth without realizing that we constantly use others for our own purposes, whatever those might be—from getting ahead in the world, to satisfying lust, to diminishing our fear of being alone, to feeling a sense of security. Even the act of giving to others is tainted with what we get from such giving. Such a view may seem cynical, but it is meant to be the starting place for exploring a view of relationships free from the constant infection of fear. Such honesty exposes the most intense fear at the heart of relationships—the fear that our capacity for loving depends on getting something for the effort.

We should not assume that there is a perfect relationship and that if only we could achieve it we would find, at least in this one place in the world, peace and contentment. Rather, let us start by facing what seems to be a fact of modern life: Relationships are becoming more and more difficult. We might, as suggested, do well to ask why we attempt them at all. Phrased another way, what is loving another person all about? If we dwell on this question, we realize that expecting relationships to be completely free of fear may be the doorway through which fears enter our connections with others, because that expectation is an illusion. It is the illusion of imagining that people are not deeply hurt, that their past has been ideal, that no trauma has touched us, that all of our troubles will disappear once we have found the right relationship. Through this opening fear gets hold of us, compels us to try to make sure we get what we need from others, and allows us to lose sight of the basic spiritual dimension of relating—that we form bonds to be of help to others, not to ourselves. We can begin to change this expectation by imagining being in a relationship exactly as we are, with all that we bring, by not expecting the relationship to heal the past, and by working to discover how we can love out of our woundedness.

Mary Reilly is a film about the household servant of Dr. Jekyll, the Dr. Jekyll of Dr. Jekyll and Mr. Hyde. A significant portion of the film shows the terrible life Mary leads as a child. Her father is monstrous to her. He drinks, beats her, and throws her into a small, dark closet, along with a sack containing a rat. Eventually, the rat eats its way out of the sack, and bites her. Mary's mother is semi-aware of this cruel treatment, but only after a rat severely bites Mary does she take her daughter and leave her husband. This story becomes known to Dr. Jekyll when he questions the deep scars on Mary's arms and neck.

Mary grows to love Dr. Jekyll, but it is a love that is not expressed romantically. Jekyll is kind to her and gradually learns more about her. When he asks whether she hates her father, she says that she does not. After years of absence, her father comes to Mary's mother's funeral and seeks to draw Mary back. She is able to stay away from this destructive relationship without hating him for what he had done.

Gradually, Mary comes to discover that Dr. Jekyll is none other than the infamous Mr. Hyde. She shows remarkable compassion for Hyde, in spite of learning that he has killed many women in the most cruel and bloody manner. Hyde lusts for her, with the insatiable lust that led him to torture and kill other women, and although Mary is afraid of him, this fear does not overtake her. She demonstrates a love for him by refusing to turn away or run, a love so powerful that he is given hope for the possibility of his own redemption.

The mood of the film carries much of the story. Nothing sentimental enters, neither in the relationship between Mary and her father nor in that between Mary and Jekyll/Hyde. A love unfolds, but it is not conventional romantic love. Spiritual love is perhaps a better term, for Mary is concerned for the soul of Hyde. A mood of emotional reserve characterizes the film, but holding back or suppressing emotion does not adequately describe the quality; the sense is more one of participating in emotions without being carried by them. Desire is present; so are attraction and fear. The only hatred is Hyde's, directed wholly toward himself.

More is going on in this film than just another version of a horror tale. With this story we see a new way to imagine relationships. First, notice that what enables Mary to love in the midst of fear are the difficult experiences of her childhood relationship with her father. Much psychological work these days assumes from the outset that individuals have difficulty with adult relationships because of fears experienced in childhood. In *Mary*

Reilly we have a picture that turns this premise up-side down.

An important aspect of this film is Mary's position as a servant. We have to take this as having more significance than a convenient role in a movie—it expresses an arche-typal reality. Mary lives within the archetypal imagination of service. Her work is more than a job. It represents a mode of being for her soul. In fact, this film is largely about selfless service. The image indicates that when we become guided by this reality, the dire circumstances of our past no longer hold us back and instead become an asset to our future encounters. This image of selfless ser-vice must be rightly understood. Such serving has its basis in thorough self-knowledge, something that Mary must have gained through years of suffering. If we try to serve another without this basis, we lose our humanity. We become only what the other wants us to be. Service must in all instances be freely given; to freely give of oneself, one must first know who one is.

The service that we see Mary engaged in goes further than that of serving the head of the estate. In one scene, she looks out into the courtyard and sees the lack of organic life there. She offers to plant flowers and herbs, and gets up early each morning to work on bringing beauty into the surroundings—and with no promise of compensation. At the beginning of the film, we see Mary washing the cobblestones in the outer entry to the house. Mary is not just in service to Dr. Jekyll; her entire life is one of service. Her service does not have the idealistic ring that one attributes to a missionary or a nurse or a doctor, nor does it have the idealism of romantic love. Mary serves not out of idealism but because that is what her life destiny has brought to her.

Relationships between human beings are evolving to the point that new purpose is now trying to appear, one that has to do with serving others. Old ways of relating, giving to others and needing a lot in return, are on their way to becoming outmoded. We think the difficulties we experience in relationships come from the fact that we are not engaged in them in the right way. Unfortunately, such a way of thinking transforms a mode of existence into a technical problem. Technique has little to do with relating; knowing who and what we are serving is what's important. Does serving mean waiting hand-and-foot on the person we love? No. It means serving the soul of the other person, not the desires and wants of that person. That Mary sees deeply into the soul of Dr. Jekyll is evident in this film—and the soul of Dr. Jekyll is none other than Mr. Hyde. Loving another person means loving the person's darkest aspects, not just the qualities that are most appealing.

When a relationship becomes focused on seeking self-gratification, we are in danger of turning into Mr. Hyde. And when self-gratification is connected with romantic ideals, sentimentalism, or religious ideology, these false pretenses become the perfect hiding place for eruptions of anger, hatred, violence, and fear.

Psychology instructs us that serving others in relationships is bad—codependence is the buzzword—and that we need to take care of ourselves first. By today's standards, Mary would definitely be considered psychologically ill. The difference is that Mary knows what she is doing, even though hers is not an intellectual knowledge but a knowing of the heart. Her attraction is to Dr. Jekyll, but her love is for Mr. Hyde. But who is Hyde, really? He is the soul of Dr. Jekyll.

If I were a therapist working with someone, what would the essence of truly helping that person be? To love his soul and look on it without judgment, so that he can experience love without reservation. I would need to enter the darkest regions, the ugliest places, the scariest dimensions of the person's soul, and do so without the slightest bit of judgment or hesitation. Such empathy constitutes an act of redemption. What would I get out of it? Nothing of a personal nature—and if I were to, the therapeutic process would get dammed up. I use the example of therapy because I believe for the past one hundred years it has been the testing ground for a new way to imagine relationships. It is now time for this imagination to enter the larger world.

Above, the therapeutic process was characterized by the single word *empathy*. This word, though, describes a process, an activity with clearly defined phases that we can practice.[3] The first aspect of this activity consists of consciously turning our attention toward another person in an attitude of openness. We extend part of our being beyond its usual boundaries, become interested in the other person's existence and destiny—but not out of curiosity, adventure, criticism, self-interest, or power. We must find this capacity within ourselves, identify it clearly. It feels like an open space, but one that we have to find, first by being aware, the best we can, of what our desires are and, in effect, releasing them. Locating this capacity is a conscious process, but it does not reside in the foreground of consciousness, which is filled with self-concerns. There must be an initial, conscious clearing of these interests, an abandoning of one's usual mental processes and a movement into an inner soul region of silence. In this clearing, you will experience a quieting of mind, an opening to the presence of the other person uncluttered by curiosity or questions. Look for it and you will find it; it is as if this clear region clicks in. You will find it by turning away from what you *think* of the other person, and at the same time turning toward a direct perception of that person.

The second aspect of this activity consists of dwelling, for a short period of time, within the inner qualities of the other person. Such experience lies more in the nature of a feeling, but does not consist of asking, "What *do I feel about* the other person?" It is more like a mood, a coloring, a sea of impressions that one dwells within in a purely receptive way, with no concern about remembering the experience. Here, you drop all your preconceived ideas about the other person. You move toward feeling the inner qualities of the other person without knowing or needing to know what they are, just as a child, before forming concepts of the world, is open to its immediate impressions and inner qualities. In this process, however, we do not for a moment lose the sense of ourselves. The exercise is not a merging with the other person.

The third phase consists in returning home to the part of ourselves we left while encountering the other person. An echo of what was experienced while dwelling within the interior of the other person remains, and this resonance now lives in us as an image of the soul. Such an inner image can gradually be brought to one's understanding through contemplation. The first two aspects often occur very quickly, in the blink of an eye. The third aspect can take seconds, hours, days, or even a lifetime.

Forming a true understanding of another person develops not as an intellectual insight but more as an inner revelation. At first, there is no language to express what we have encountered. Words come slowly because we cannot apply our own concepts to the experience but rather must allow the image-experience to speak. The inner image teaches us the language that expresses it best.

The exercise develops the conscious capacity to relate to the soul life of others. Such an activity frees the soul from fear because, rather than using the other person to calm our fears, which is so often the case in relationships, we are called out of ourselves to be present to the other person.

Developing the capacity for empathy is a new form of education, an education into the conscious art of relating. Reading the description of this process above, one might feel that it is strange and decidedly uncomfortable. Why can't we just follow our attractions, form bonds based on those attractions, work through the difficulties as they arise, and if the difficulties cannot be worked out, either dissolve the bond or go to an expert who can show us how to proceed successfully? Unfortunately, all of the psychological tricks for relating occupy us only with trying to learn the tricks of the game, which can be satisfying for a time, but which ultimately leave the dark qualities of the other person and of our own soul lonely and isolated. When we keep ourselves apart from the true inner qualities of the other person, and separate from our own soul capacities, fear can enter more deeply into the life of relationships, safely hidden within clever psychological techniques. If we are not capable of loving all aspects of another person, we are equally unable to love all aspects of ourselves, especially the darkness in our own souls.

Fear of Suffering and Death

We are becoming more accustomed to hearing reports of near-death experiences. We are all familiar with the image of the tunnel, with the words "go toward the light," with meeting family members who have crossed the threshold, with angelic beings, with meeting Christ. For many people today, death is seen not as an end but as a transition from one form of existence to another. While such stories remain on the fringes of the consciousness of most people, as a culture we are undoubtedly confronting the fear of death more fully and creatively than ever before. The stages of coming to terms with death are now so well known that most of us can recite them by heart, and the proliferation of books on death and dying signals the development of a healthy psychology of death and the entry of a spiritual imagination into the general culture.

We may not be so afraid of death as we are terrified of what might precede it.

We seem now to be more afraid of the pain and suffering surrounding death than we are of death itself. In other words, fear no longer wears the mask of death, but of suffering. The two are not very far apart, of course, and the shift may be no more than a diabolical sleight of hand on the part of fear. Once we know in our very flesh and bones that we are dying, or going to die, once we have experienced the all-pervading, undeniable dread, then fear is defeated. Once we believe that death is not an end, fear is similarly defeated. So, the fear of death backs up a bit, to where it still has a point of attack, and infects with its sting in a different form. It enters our imagination as the possibility of horrible pain and lingering suffering.

The fear of death has never had to do with the feeling that it would be a painful event. Death taunts us with the fear that perhaps our entire life—everything we have done, felt, and thought—may, in the final analysis, be of no significance. Thus, those who live without an inner certainty of why we are here or where we are going experience a terrible dread of death. This is fear's entry point into the phenomenon of death. Only when one fails to live deeply with the question of the meaning of one's life, though, can the fear of death supersede the fear of pain and suffering.

While we may be more prepared for death, we are simply not ready, at the level of soul, for bodily pain and suffering. If life is lived without truly feeling the presence of the beauty in the world, which is an experience of both awe and pain, we are weak in our capacity to confront the intensity of feeling that characterizes suffering. The pain of suffering looms so large, in other words, because the wonder of feeling has not been cultivated. In a large part, the fear of suffering expresses a more hidden fear: that in spite of having denied it for most of our lives, we will eventually experience real feeling. Perhaps such feeling will be compressed into a very short period, especially if it has been neglected for a very long time. The price of this neglect is dear, however. When feeling bursts forth at the end of life, it lacks the context of beauty, and can often be experienced only as anguish.

Cultivating feeling in life is no guarantee that pain and suffering will be absent at the end. But under such circumstances pain and suffering cannot hold the power of breaking the soul and spirit so that nothing remains but a dark abyss. Here, we come to a most important distinction, that there are two fundamental kinds of fear. First, there is fear that presents itself as terror, which separates us from our soul life, and from vital, living connection with others and the world at large. And then there is fear that presents itself as awe, which fills us with wonder and makes us aware of our human deficiencies. The first is unholy fear, while the latter is holy fear. The work of freeing the soul from fear seeks the transformation of unholy terror and the embrace of holy fear. How well we have done in this transformation and embrace may become evident only when we are faced with our earthly ending. We get hints, though, in the way we imagine suffering. Does our imagination of suffering carry a foreboding doom, or does an inextinguishable light shine at the center of this darkness?

Modern medicine looks on pain as a technical problem. The majority of today's physicians put forth the view that pain can be managed, primarily through drugs. Others believe that some pain cannot be managed and offer death as a remedy, kindly called doctor-assisted suicide. Neither group sees any value in suffering itself, and both views have a one-sided sense of pain, limiting it to the physical realm. With such an outlook, intense feeling becomes unbearable because the spirit is easily broken. The individuals who care for those in pain have themselves lost their own direct sense of soul and have denied the reality of spirit. Not knowing what to do, they can only offer technical help in the form of morphine or assisted suicide.

Painful suffering moves one into isolation—away from others and the surrounding world. Only one reality remains, that of suffering, and in that reality the patient is totally alone. The loneliness one suffers often seems unbridgeable, and it may appear that the only way to assist the patient is to become insensitive at the soul level. All physicians undergo a discipline early in their training that shuts them off from their feelings in the presence of someone in pain. Confronted with a reality over which they have no control, they concentrate solely on the practical concerns of what can be done. How many doctors sit with a patient in pain, grieving with her, crying out in anguish, feeling her suffering as if it were their own? The soul life of the patient is thus abandoned. Perhaps the hospital chaplain comes in to offer the consolation of the spirit, but he will likely keep a distance, safely insulated behind kind and gentle words from participating in the suffering. Loved ones may grieve and cry, but usually they do so as an expression of their own pain, not together with the suffering person.

Being left to suffer in this manner, completely alone, is what we semiconsciously imagine will happen to us and what inspires fear, a fear that lives within us on a daily basis, of which we are hardly aware. The original intention of the Hospice movement was to address the isolating circumstances of suffering more than to help patients cope with pain. Although there are many Hospice workers with a remarkable capacity to relate intimately with the suffering and dying, I am aware, having sat in on a number of Hospice staff meetings, that the medical attitude has come to dominate. Many Hospice workers simply cannot, on their own, sustain intimacy with the dying person, and back away. Staff meetings become medical reports, where pain management dominates the conversation, distance is gained, and no one is willing or able to find the proper language to help the group as a whole learn how to stay with the suffering.

A wonderful archetypal story of being with another in pain is found in the Greek drama *Philoctetes*. The title character was on his way to Troy with Agamemnon and Menelaus. They got off their ship at the tiny island of Chryse to sacrifice to the local gods. As he was walking up to the shrine, Philoctetes was bitten by a viper. The wound became infected, turned black, and soon was a raging, bleeding sore. Eventually, pus and rot attracted maggots to the wound, which filled the air with a stench that no man could stomach. His companions, nauseated from the sight and smell of him, took Philoctetes from Chryse and left him on the deserted island of Lemnos. There was no life whatsoever on that island—no trees, plants, or animals—only dry earth and rocky crags. Philoctetes would not have survived except for a bow and arrow given to him by Heracles. The hero had received that bow from Apollo himself and gave it to Philoctetes

as he was dying. The bow was a remarkable instrument—
it never missed the mark, such was its precision. Precious
few birds flew over Lemnos, but Philoctetes never
missed a shot and he was able to survive, though just
barely.

For ten years, Philoctetes suffered alone on the island,
his maggot-ridden foot never healing, and only a dead
bird to eat from time to time. Filled with bitterness, rage,
and loneliness, Philoctetes gave up on humankind and the
gods alike. Then one day a ship approached. Odysseus and
a youth, Neoptolemus, son of Achilles, stepped onto
shore. They had come to retrieve Philoctetes, for an ora-
cle had prophesied that Troy would be conquered only
with his help. Their plan had been to trick him into coming with them, but as Neoptolemus talked with Philoctetes he quickly gave up his ruse. He admired the courage
of this suffering individual, and instead of trying to
manipulate him, he waited with Philoctetes, heard his
stories, cared for him, cried out with him. Odysseus
stayed in the background, watching from afar, but finally
entered and threatened to force Philoctetes to leave.
Philoctetes grabbed the bow and was about to shoot
Odysseus. Suddenly, Heracles appeared in a vision,
telling Philoctetes that he must go to Troy. There he would
recover his health and obtain glory.

In the midst of our daily labors of life, we may suddenly

succumb to a serious illness and be taken off to the hospital, much as Philoctetes, in the midst of carrying out his duties, was stricken and taken to the island of Lemnos. The name Philoctetes means "love of possessions," and on that deserted island he found himself deprived of everything, his bow and arrow being his only lifeline. Each of us, if we become gravely ill, is just as suddenly deprived of everything that gives us a sense of who we are. Everything we possess is stripped from us. Visitors may arrive, coming to express their sympathy, asking how we feel today, and then talking about everything that is going on at home, how much we are missed, how the people at work cannot wait until we are back on the job. If we are lucky, not every visitor who comes is so uncomfortable at the sight of our suffering that he diverts attention from the intense reality onto other subjects. At least one person, we hope, is able to lament, mourn, cry out with us in our suffering, and indeed help us enter it even more deeply.

The appearance of Heracles in a vision, urging Philoctetes to return to the human community where he will recover health and receive glory, should not, of course, be taken literally. This image appears as a companion to the compassionate presence of Neoptolemus as a way of saying that Philoctetes can return to the community because someone shares his pain and suffering.

When one is allowed to speak, to cry, to despair, to mourn, to grieve, without having to be concerned with putting words together in response to the demands of others, then a community of suffering forms, the isolation is broken, and fear can no longer take over.

If pain is only a physical reality, then perhaps it is justified to use any means to curtail it. But the soul also expresses itself within pain, and excessive dulling of pain also obscures the soul and makes access to the spirit impossible. Pain has to do with the nerve processes of the body. In normal life, when we are well, the nerve processes function in smooth relation with the life processes, and we feel a vitality in the organs of the body—the lungs, liver, spleen, stomach, and so on. Soul processes are also reflected in the organs of the body and are thus intimately related to the life processes. The relationship between the life processes and soul processes is not recognized in current physiology or psychology, but it was well known in earlier times. For example, alchemy and early forms of medicine pictured a definite relationship between the planets and particular organs of the body. The Renaissance philosopher Marsilio Ficino directly related the planets to the life of the soul.[4]

Normally, a wonderful balance and harmony maintains between the nerve processes and the life processes, a relationship that becomes disturbed in illness. When there is some dysfunction of the organs, the life processes create an intense stimulation of the nerve processes, which is experienced as pain. Intense stimulation of the nerve processes is merely a technical way of saying that soul life erupts into consciousness without the mediation of images. This understanding of pain comes from the work of Rudolf Steiner[5] and research in anthroposophical medicine.[6] Such an understanding strongly suggests that how we bear our pain may have a great deal to do with what kind of soul work we have done during our life. It also suggests that relating at a soul level to those who suffer pain—grieving, mourning, crying, not for but with the suffering—may be as important as the technical measures we employ to alleviate pain. Participating at the level of soul frees the sufferer from trying to satisfy the subtle demands of those around him. Such engagement also allows for the expression of the soul that may have been neglected for years—the sorrows, regrets, unlived hopes and dreams, desires, unresolved conflicts, misunderstandings, and most important, all the fears that still linger and become intensified when confronted with our mortality.

We are able to be of service to those who suffer only to the extent that we have been able to transform fear in our own lives. Such efforts of the soul also prepare us for the painful suffering that we may encounter ourselves.

Perhaps we will be able to work in the right way with technical solutions to pain, able to be aware when medications go too far and begin to obliterate subtle aspects of the full mystery of pain. Eliminating pain medication is certainly not suggested here. Rather, I am suggesting the importance of considering the soul in relation to pain and making sure that this factor is not extinguished altogether. If we know that others will be with us at the level of soul in times of suffering, much of the fear surrounding pain can be overcome.

CHAPTER 5

The Ecology of Fear

Until recent times—I myself mark the change as occurring at 8:15 A.M. on August 6, 1945, the moment of the explosion of the atomic bomb over Hiroshima—a threshold existed between our everyday world of experiences and the worlds of fear. Since then, a threshold no longer exists, as if that mushroom cloud spread throughout the world, settling in permanently.[1] The bomb was proof of a radical separation; it announced our renunciation of the world as a sacred place. Fear certainly existed before this time, but its outbreaks seemed controllable through a combination of law, religious sensibility, psychiatric treatment, political negotiation, and most of all, denial. Never before had it become emboldened enough to come out into the open so clearly, though it had prepared to do so earlier in the form of Hitler. The question is not whether there is more dread in the world today than there used to be; probably not. But never before has it existed so separate from a context of understanding the sacred character of the universe.

Fear constitutes a much larger and more comprehensive presence than has yet been realized. Beginning in the nineteenth century, therapeutic psychology sought to identify the symptoms related to this phenomenon. The types of fear recognized included hysteria, behind which some trauma, real or imagined, was always to be found; shell shock or combat neurosis, now commonly called post-traumatic stress syndrome, which was first investigated after World War I; abuse and domestic violence; fear of natural catastrophes such as earthquakes, hurricanes, tornadoes, or fire; individual phobias such as panic attacks, anxieties, and obsessive-compulsive disorders.

The reality of fear is far more wide-ranging, however. Working with victims of trauma does little to impede the larger presence of fear in the world. The goal is to become more conscious of what we are dealing with and to recognize that different fears require different capacities of soul to overcome them. The need is not to remove fear from the world, but instead to develop in ourselves the psychic capacity to confront its destructive power. In this realm, consciousness, coupled with love, is everything.

Enlarging consciousness to include an awareness of soul allows a healthy struggle with fear, and love makes possible its transformation, not just within ourselves but also within the world.

A distinction might be drawn between the personal dimensions of fear and the appearance of fear as an archetypal reality. If, for example, one is afraid to walk down the street at night because gangs have become a menace to the neighborhood, this emotion is a personal response. Jung's psychology, and the archetypal psychology of James Hillman as well, would look deeper into the phenomenon to find the archetypal image behind this personal reaction. In Greek myth, for instance, Phobos is the god of fear, while Pan is the god of panic. The reason for cringing in the face of a shadowy figure running toward you in the dark, both Jung and his successors would agree, is due to the presence of Phobos or Pan or some other god, not in the world but within the soul or psyche.[2] Jung's psychology has provided an invaluable contribution in recognizing the objective character of the psyche. In his view, our subjective states are the result of the mediating activity of the soul, which is constantly expressing archetypal images.

Today, however, psychic reality encompasses both inner states and the outer world, and archetypal imagination has now become part of the world. The collapse of the boundary between the world and the presence of fear in it has introduced these archetypes into our daily experience, which previously occurred only in our darkest dreams and in pathological states. Now it is as if we live our waking lives in a kind of dream world. Archetypal images don't always inspire fear, of course, but fearful images appear to have enough force to venture beyond inner psychic experience and show up in the outer world.

Examples of the confluence of our everyday reality with a more fearful, imaginal world are so pervasive that we hardly notice this merging has happened. And yet there is evidence of this odd union in the surreal quality that accompanies fearful events. Think, for example, of the eerie quality surrounding the crash of an airliner; or the unbelievable quality of seeing the terrorist bombing of a building on the news; or the skin-crawling experience of learning that a person down the street has shot his family. This quality also characterizes more individual experiences of fear. Think of the strange way the world changes with a personal emergency—a child nearly drowning, being told that a loved one has been rushed to the hospital, being in a car crash.

Perception occurs through the senses, cognition through the mind, and archetypal images through the soul. Because the channels for world perception and cognition are different from the channel for soul awareness, perception and cognition adjust pretty well to the invasion of these fearful images. We still perceive everything around us as sure and steady, and attribute increasing instabilities to human factors. If, for example, fear looms on the streets of the city, it must be due to drug trafficking, flight to the suburbs, economic factors, loss of community. If the fear of war grips us, it must be due to nationalistic impulses and political struggles. If we are alarmed by the thousands of jobs lost every year from corporate downsizing, we attribute our anxiety to changing economic conditions. Fear is not seen as the archetypal force creating these devastations.

It would be wonderfully liberating, indeed, if we were able to admit that we are all tremendously afraid. That would be the first step in recognizing that healthy terror can be the beginning of wisdom. When we realize that we are in a world governed by fear and that we do not know what is out there any more than earlier explorers knew what awaited them across the oceans, we can begin to explore the geography of this new world. Let us see now what we can achieve by approaching fear from this attitude of exploration.

Fear in the Physical World

In dreams, things intermingle that in the ordinary world do not. Each fragment by itself may be recognizable, but when they occur together, we experience them according to the logic of images, and not of the natural world. We say a dream has an certain archetypal quality when a dominant value threads its way through the unrelated pictures of dream life. When, for example, someone dreams of standing on a street looking into a window in which there is a display of bathing suits, and simultaneously a beautiful woman walks by, leaving a waft of perfume behind, then the dream expresses the archetypal quality of Aphrodite. The goddess does not show up directly in the dream, but her beauty and sensuality are present in the dream image as a whole.

Likewise, when we observe things in the physical world associated with different fears, at first they may seem to be separate and unrelated. Nonetheless, fearful events and objects all exude a similar aura, and if we concentrate on that aura, these separate elements form a common landscape of images. Thus, significant world events that may initially seem unrelated—nuclear testing in France, India, and Pakistan; an Alaskan oil spill; the smog over Mexico City, Los Angeles, or any major city of the world; global warming; floods and earthquakes; forest fires—coalesce into a unified imagination. This imagination is that the Earth is steeped in fear.

What makes this picture so terrifying? I've come to the conclusion that rather than a fearful presence, it is an absence that makes this image horrifying. What this picture lacks is love. It is as if we have been inserted into a world in which the caring presence of love has been removed and chaos reigns.

Love exists in the very substance of matter, it is what binds the world together as a whole, a form of attraction between things. We may not see it, but it is there. Love is an objective quality of the world. The form it takes in matter doesn't have anything to do with our feelings or sentiments, although it can be removed by what we do or don't do in relation to the world. Another way to speak of the absence of love is that certain spiritual presences— traditionally called angels, elemental beings, fairies, or spirits of place—have departed from the scene.

As fear comes to dominate the world, the natural love that resides in the individual soul also withers and dies. The soul dreads the loss of its own existence. For the soul, severe and forbidding images are not in themselves scary. What's terrifying is the possibility of existing without the quality of love, for love is the soul's way of knowing its own being. In the myth of Eros and Psyche, it is the presence of Eros that makes it possible for Psyche to come to self-knowledge, for soul to know herself. Such myths picture profound truths. The feeling of love is the soul's verification of its own existence. Fear's entry in such strong ways into the physical world is the equivalent to the loss of soul. Love then wanders around confused, with no place to rest.

Are we really justified in saying love exists within the physical world, as part of the oceans and rivers, the air with the mists and clouds, the crust of the earth with its plains, mountains, valleys, stones, metals, crystals, deserts, hills, canyons? Have I merely introduced sentiment in order to capture your feelings? The physical world always seems to offer itself, seeking nothing in return, providing beauty, comfort, strength, solidity, enjoyment, grandeur. It is our foundation and serves us in every way. Still, we might argue that these same qualities can be described in purely scientific terminology without resorting to the language of emotions. To do so, however, requires absenting one's soul from any act of perceiving the world and relies on viewing the world through the eyes of the natural sciences, coldly, analytically. To perceive love in the world, on the other hand, is to see the world as a revelation of spiritual presences, spiritual beings. Ancient mythical consciousness felt the world to be such a revelation; there were spiritual beings who maintained the flowing water of springs, nymphs of caverns and caves, guardian spirits of hills and mountains, spirits of the air.

We cannot, of course, return to ancient modes of consciousness where such beings could be directly perceived. Apprehending spiritual presences no longer concerns the content of perception, but deals with *how* we perceive, and with understanding the sensory and psychic acts that forge our connection with the world. If we approach the world as holy, as sacred, as consecrated, instead of merely a collection of material objects, then more subtle qualities reveal themselves. Perception is a moral act, an act of devotion toward the world, not just a physiological process that occurs automatically.[3]

Suppose I drive to a giant redwood forest in northern California. I leave the car at the edge of the forest and walk in. Quite suddenly, an immense stillness comes over the surroundings. Even the birds are hushed. The colors—greens, browns, reds, grays—are at the same time softer and more vivid than those outside this landscape. My companion and I speak with each other, and without intending to do so, we find ourselves whispering. A holiness pervades the place; we are walking in a living temple. Many have had just this experience, and it arises from a moral perception. In behaving in this way we are acting in harmony with what is around us. It is, of course, possible to act otherwise. But by doing so, the subtle perceptual qualities in the surroundings would begin to disappear. The existence of fear in a physical place destroys the sacredness of that place. Places that still exude magical presences seem less and less able to maintain their specialness. People are often unable to respond to the holiness of a place such as a redwood forest. They are littered with trash, trampled, or made available for clear-cutting.

For us to be fully conscious, the moral dimension of perception must be developed. In ordinary sensory experience, this dimension exists only as a potential, and its actualization depends on our taking up the task of ensouling the senses. Rudolf Steiner has given detailed exercises for the development of the moral, soul qualities of perceiving.[4] These practices, when carried out over time, begin to reveal the physical world as pervaded with creative presences. Steiner suggests, for example, that if one concentrates all of one's attention on the blue expanse of the sky, excluding all else from consciousness—all other external impressions, all memories, all thoughts—then something happens after a few moments. A certain soul mood arises, a feeling of devotion. This feeling is not a subjective state, but an actual perception, a moral perception of what lives in the expanse of blue. He then suggests exercises for perceiving similar qualities that exist in streams, the ocean, clouds, and mist. Engaging in such practices sensitizes the soul to the deeper qualities within the physical world and alleviates fear, because we can again experience a love-filled universe.

Daily life itself can become the place to practice the

development of moral perception. All we need to do is to be more receptive and let the things of the world completely fill our consciousness, holding in abeyance the willful encroachment of our thinking into our surroundings. Gradually, a soul mood of holiness comes through strongly along with whatever we are perceiving. Seeing the world through the developed capacities of soul not only reveals more of what is there but also invites back the spiritual presences that have receded because of the literal-minded way we have come to view the world.

We need soul ecology to accompany physical ecology. Our concern has to include the elemental beings of trees, lakes, and plants, along with the actual things themselves. The organ of perception that can sense these invisible beings is the soul. Soul capacities first have to be activated by locating the creative power of love within each of us. The task now is to create this factor from within, out of an effort of pure will. The will-to-love resides in the deepest recesses of the soul. This power of the soul can be discovered by each and every individual; it often comes to light only at our darkest moments, when all else has been stripped away. This desire is not a love for this or a love for that; it is without content and without object, a pure effulgence in the heart of darkness.

Fear in the Life Processes

When we observe life forms in the natural world, we see that they are threatened. Examples of this can be over-whelming—they are so large and so pervasive that they numb us into feeling we can do nothing about them. Radioactivity continues to pose a hazard to all life forms; chemical pesticides and fertilizers are used almost universally in farming; artificial hormones cause cows to overproduce milk; ultraviolet radiation due to ozone depletion is a threat to sensitive creatures such as frogs. My purpose in naming these is not to produce numbing, but to expose the clustering of fears around many varied life forms. Such a diagnosis is needed if we are to find the right ways to respond.

Nothing in soul life occurs without a sympathetic vibration shooting through the life processes of the body. A primary life process is breathing, by which a body's inner life is supported from the outside. I refer here not only to the breathing characteristic of human life but also to the exchanges occurring between all life forms and the surrounding element of air. A second life process is warmth, by which a living body maintains a certain temperature necessary for life. A further life process is nour-ishment, through which the life of a body enters into relationships with the world so that substances used are replaced. Another life process is secretion, a process necessary, for example, for eating and digestion. A fifth process is the transformation of nutrients so that they can serve to build up the physical body of living beings. A sixth process is that of growing, and the final one is reproducing.[5] These life activities vary considerably, ranging from a single-cell organism to plant life, animal life, and human life, but something of these processes is found wherever life expresses itself. All these biological actions, individually and as a whole, are now immersed in fear.

One would think that fear in the realm of the life processes would be easier to understand than fear in the physical world, but it is quite the opposite. Here, suddenly, fear becomes a part of us, without a separation marking it as over there and us as over here. Such intense anxiety enters that it cannot be tolerated for very long. A creepy feeling comes over us when we consider the degree to which our bodies exist within a toxic environment. An intense desire for control seizes us, which is exactly what fear in this domain seems to anticipate. We attempt to gain a modicum of control by looking at all of these things and, in effect, live in denial of them. We gain illusory control by pretending such things are not affecting us because we do not feel them physically. Or we become skeptical; where is the proof that these factors are really harmful? Or we become cynical and angry, feeling nothing can be done.

If we pause and think for a moment, does it seem possible that radiation penetrating all life forms, chemicals of all sorts in our food, and scientists working to reduce us to strings of biochemicals would not instill unremitting horror in us? Fear of this nature offers the illusion that we can control any dire effects wrought upon us and the world through technical achievements. We become fascinated with the illusion of power. It is as if fear says that as we yield to its control over us, it will in turn give us power over the world, as if it allows us to believe that this control will be beneficial.

For example, if the gene responsible for a particular kind of mental retardation can be found, we then have control over that malady. But the possibility that the retardation came about through a change over time in the quality of a certain food as a result of promoting its growth through some chemical goes completely unnoticed. Thus, fear does not lose its foothold in the world. In fact, it is free to make further advances as we become more fascinated with our power to control, and lose sight of why we sought that power in the first place.

To take another example, the proliferation of electronic technology offers control over information. This seems to be a good thing. Never mind the possibility that your eyes are being direly affected by the radiation streaming out of the computer screen. The effects may not be evident for generations, and by that time we perhaps will have found the gene that can be manipulated to counter such exposure. Anyone who proposes today that many of our technological advances may not be safe has no way to prove their assertions since the effects are subtle and require generations to manifest themselves. Such people are accused of trying to impede the march of progress.

As the life processes of the world are interfered with, and the vitality of the human body erodes, disruption of the living relationship between the vital, natural world and the cosmos takes place. Plant life, for example, begins to take its course independently of the sky, the clouds, the sun, the moon, the rain, and even the planets and the stars. Organic life becomes disconnected from the conditions of the cosmos. Nature becomes subnatural. A partial process now has the appearance of being a whole and complete process. The growth of plants seems to depend on conditions of the soil, chemicals, and fertilizers only, whereas healthy plant life is the interdependent relation of soil, air, water, light, atmosphere, and even the position of the sun, the moon, and the planets. Further, since the human body participates in the life processes of the world, the body is separated from the life of the cosmos as these processes are disrupted. This separation is felt as anxiety.

Electromagnetic energy furthers the process of devitalizing the organic world and the vital processes of the body. There is much evidence that diseases such as cancer and leukemia may result from exposure to electrical fields. Farmers in Wisconsin and other places have reported that cows' milk production is severely damaged by power lines running across farmlands, an observation vehemently denied by the power companies. Electrical energy now bounces throughout the universe, and who knows its long-range effects.

It is not possible to avoid participating in this deadly trap. If I eat only organic food, avoid television, telephones, computers, cellular phones, the Internet, I am not exempt from the pressures and effects of modern life. The only all-important element is consciousness. Cultivating an awareness of our situation is the first step out of fear. When we stop living in denial of the world's dangers, then a second step becomes possible—recognizing the soul's engagement with these realms of fear. A concrete involvement with the balancing factors of soul life is an absolute prerequisite to finding real, not illusory, ways of being free of fear.

As an exercise for reengaging soul life, take a small potted plant. Look closely at the plant, seeing all its details, but also observe the form as a whole. Then close your eyes and make an exact inner image of the plant. Build the image piece by piece. If you close your eyes and try to make an inner image of the entire plant, it will not be a precise image, but either an abstract idea or a vague memory of what you saw. Instead, close your eyes and build up the stem and one leaf. Then open your eyes and look again. Upon closing your eyes, add the next leaf of the plant. Continue doing this until the complete image has been constructed. Naturally, as this is being done it is necessary to let go of any other images or thoughts that try to intrude. Once the image has been built up, hold it stable for a few moments. Do not let it fade away or take on other qualities or shift into anything else. Then, in your imagination, start removing the plant-image by removing each leaf, one by one, starting with the leaf that was added last and proceeding in the reverse order to the previous construction. When all the leaves have been removed, then remove the stalk. At this point there is a void. Hold this void for a few moments, listening into the emptiness.

The emptiness does not remain blank. A kind of feeling of the force-field of the plant arises, sometimes taking the form of moving rays of light. It is as if you can feel the invisible forces all around that create the form of this particular plant. This quality of feeling characterizes the life force of the plant.[6]

A small act such as this performed a few minutes a day builds the imaginative capacities of the soul to be present to the fullness of life forms. You will notice that immediate perception of the outer world begins to change. You become present to details, their nuances, their subtleties, as if seeing them for the first time. Colors appear less harsh, owing to an increased sensitivity to the play of light and shadow. The forms of different plants are seen in a new way. The gesture of the leaves of one plant are like outstretched palms of the hand, open to the sky above. The leaves of another are like hands folded in a gesture of prayer, while another reaches downward with its leaves, as if in praise of the earth. Trees are seen as majestic pillars of strength, reaching simultaneously toward the sky and deep into the earth, uniting the air above and the soil below. Life becomes less abstract and more of a living reality that can be sensed directly. It is as if something has been added back into the world. We are not projecting, but rather seeing what is actually there because we approach it with the proper capacities. If soul is excluded from our perception, then we see things only partially.

Imagination is a real force, not just a subjective inner state. More crucial, it is a *moral* force. As we begin to operate from our imagination's connection to the outer world, fear diminishes, because we are returning to life forms what has been taken away. We recognize that this is taking place because our own level of fear and anxiety gradually diminishes. Our capacity for conscious imagination, joined with the world, is a primary tool for overcoming fear.

Fear in the Feeling World

A third sphere invaded by fear is the world of feeling. The main indication that our feeling life has been split apart is found in the way we consider feeling. We look at it now as a possession—I have my feelings about this or that, and they are all mine. We have completely personalized a domain that rightly belongs together with the surrounding world. Once feeling is torn from an ongoing, sensual, embodied relation with the world, the need to feel becomes an insatiable addiction, or it disappears altogether. When the latter is the case, feeling will usually erupt in some kind of symptom, such as severe depression or outbreaks of uncontrollable anger.

The subjectivizing of feeling signifies a flight from the sensuous world, prompted by the full-fledged entrance of fear into the feeling world. When our participation with the world is disrupted, feeling begins to seem like a quantifiable item. We are given "designer" feelings— programmed sensations that simulate a connection to the sensuous presence of the world, but typically in far more intense forms. We go to the movies, are moved to tears, laughter, joy, sadness, disgust, rage, eroticism. We listen to music that stirs emotions chaotically. We are assaulted by advertising that arouses the idea that certain feeling states can be had if only we buy the object advertised. Packets of feeling can be purchased in the form of drugs on a street corner. Pornography is available to excite every form of sexual feeling imaginable. Psychotherapies are available to help us to feel our feelings rather than to feel the world.

The fear inherent in these kinds of escapes has to do with the confusion of feeling with sensation. Feeling is not sensation. The quantification of feeling sensational-izes the everyday world and transmutes spiritual qualities into materialistic properties. We search for feeling, and what we get is a sensation, a quick fix—at the heavy metal concert, in the movie theater, rolled into a reefer, designed by Calvin Klein, in a video store, in a support group, with a quick burger and fries. On the surface, these all seem to be pleasures. But the element of fear is not hard to detect.

Fear lives in the midst of such sensations as a constant feeling of unsettledness and unfulfillment, and later as a deadening emptiness following one's withdrawal from the experience. This emptiness ranges from a vague, unlocatable gnawing presence to a raw, cold, shuddering fear. While this terrifying void may seem to originate from the absence of the desired sensation, the void is actually an inherent part of the sensation itself but is usually masked by the physiological excitation that passes as feeling. In other words, our feeling relation with the world has been replaced by a heightened experience of our own biological activity.

As the feeling life collapses into sensations, the life of the senses is overwhelmed and thrown out of balance. Another dimension of fear enters through this overstimulation as certain senses are constantly aroused while others are completely neglected. The senses that give us the most immediate experience of our body—the sense of touch, the sense of movement, the sense of balance—tend to be overstimulated. Overwhelming these senses results in a paralyzing of the will; we are not able to move in harmonious ways; we feel as if we are being pushed and shoved around. When the senses that connect us to the surrounding world—vision, smell, warmth, taste, hearing—are overstimulated, we lose the ability to experience the soul qualities of the things of the world. Beyond these are even more subtle senses: one having to do with sensing qualities in speech and another having to do with perceiving directly the soul qualities of other human beings. These are often completely overwhelmed, to the point that most people are not even aware that they have such senses.

The terror of investing so much of our lives in sensation shows up as obsession, for we really cannot live without feeling. If it is not available as an ongoing relation with the soul qualities of the world, then its substitutes will be sought with such forcefulness that nothing can stop them. The horror of obsessiveness is that while it can be momentarily quieted, it cannot be resolved.[7] The satisfaction of an urge does not result in consciousness, but rather in just the opposite, the dimming of consciousness into a kind of waking dream state. If I become obsessed with a person and cannot seem to live without her, the presence of the person does not result in a conscious relationship, but rather in a temporary lulling and forgetfulness of my desire. If the person must be present for me to feel comfortable, the sensation of the person may calm me for a while. But those sensations will wane, and no matter what the person does I will complain that she is not really present, even when nearby, for my soul feeling is numb. If I become obsessed with shopping, giving in to the urge to buy things renders me less conscious, not more. Again, the sensation of buying and having can be momentarily comforting. However, that sensation is not real feeling and depends on a contingency, the physical presence of a thing.

Counterfeit feeling is a result of believing that events, substances, or commodities are able to produce wondrous states within us. It makes it possible to sense contentment even when I am not content in soul, to feel warmth toward others when I have not worked to bring warmth into our relationship, to feel transcendence when I am merely overstimulating my senses. If, for example, music is strongly amplified through electronic means, the vibrations work right into the flesh and bones so that the music is made palpable and is experienced as touch. If light and color are greatly intensified, as they are in certain movies, it is as if one is immersed in color and can feel it as well as see it. This kind of synesthesia is a pre-rational experience, something similar to what infants experience before the separation of the senses is completed. It is not a spiritual experience, even though it is often confused with one.[8] In a highly abstract culture such as ours, easily acquired synesthesia-like experiences seem to be transcendental experiences because they momentarily take us out of dry rationalistic thought. They are the exact opposite.

How might we offset the pervasiveness of fear that has entered the feeling world? The heart of the problem of feeling, surprisingly, lies in the way that we know the world. We cannot feel in healthy ways because our cognition is disordered. Feeling always has a cognitive aspect; feelings are ways of knowing, a knowing through the soul.[9] Sensations, however, lack the inner reflectiveness of feeling. If cognition does not already contain an element of feeling, any movement toward feeling will be eclipsed by nonreflective sensation. Cognition ought to begin with a theosophical imagination of the world—an imagination of the world as a revelation of the spiritual worlds. As long as we see the world only as material husks, our way of knowing is centered in something dead: abstract thought. But if the world reveals the working of spiritual beings—if every rock, every tree, every animal is a living composite of spirit and matter, life and death, cold and warm, sweet and bitter—then feeling is at the very heart of the world. The fundamental quality within the world, from which all other feelings originate like branches of a great tree, is reverence. Rather than conceiving of the world as dead matter, atoms, electric particles, let us conceive of the world as soul embodied.

In the arena of our desires and instincts, what tends to be lacking most is receptivity. Grasping, wanting, and needing are so strong that patience, waiting, and allowing can hardly be felt unless consciously cultivated. Such balance can be gradually achieved, however, through developing an inner silence while observing the outer world. This kind of observation is not a scientific, detached observation, but warmth-filled interest. In scientific observation, one relates to the world ascetically, setting aside any emotion that might disturb one's objectivity. In a knowing that is at the same time feeling, one brings desire and instinct to bear on what one is observing—but not in the disturbing way in which they usually rumble within us. The rumbling is brought to silence through meditative concentration, through learning to become still within oneself. Desire and instinct gradually become transformed into interest. Speaking psychologically, we might say that libido flows freely into the world instead of being turned inward, where it simultaneously creates self-feeling disconnected from the world and the need to resolve the disturbances it engenders.

When we look at the world in a detached manner, emotional life becomes dammed up. While producing the illusion that feeling is our possession, it also produces cruelty. When even the most supposedly delicate feeling—such as an urge to comfort or give affection to another person—originates not out of an ongoing relation with the world but from stirred-up instincts and passions, it can turn from care to violence in the blink of an eye.

How is it possible to bring waiting, patience, and receptivity to bear on the urges of instincts and passions when we do not seem to have any control whatsoever over these subconscious aspects of our being? It is not something that can be done directly. I cannot will my desires to be in conscious relation to the world. We do, however, have some control over our thoughts. We can occupy our minds with pure and noble ideas. We can read and meditate on things that are spiritually nourishing and inspiring. We can read and contemplate the works of the great masters and saints who have trod the path before us to gain an understanding of how they confronted the difficult matters we have considered here. In such contemplative work, we not only gain knowledge and understanding but also experience a palpable sense that we are being aided in our efforts by those who have struggled and succeeded before. An inner strength, beyond what we could ourselves muster, inspires us. Such thoughts then work indirectly in the realm of our instincts and passions, refining them. We can also, in small ways, work toward the benefit of others rather than seek always to indulge ourselves. In this way, indirectly, passion and instinct are transformed. They are not annihilated, nor are they repressed. Rather, they become the vehicle and the medium for feeling engagement with the world.

CHAPTER 6

_____

The Double

Why do we not experience fear far more forcefully and continually than we do? Have we become so accustomed to it that it does not really bother us except when encountered with an intensity we cannot ignore? Are we really that numb? Numbness in relation to fears does not stem from repression but from something far more serious—a situation in which we have become co-conspirators with fear without even knowing it has taken place. When this happens the very essence of a person is replaced by something that looks and acts exactly like a person but is not.

We are not always ourselves. This fact is well known, and the study and treatment of people who have trouble being themselves is a field of therapeutic psychology.

Freud identified psychic mechanisms such as denial, projection, and displacement as defenses against aspects of ourselves that seem unacceptable. In extreme instances, when what lies beneath the surface of consciousness cannot be tolerated, Freud theorized that a person would form an alter-ego. Jung put forth the view that when we are removed from the inner, spontaneous, image-making activity originating within the soul, we become split off from the fullness of ourselves. The unsavory aspects of ourselves stay buried within us, he said, and form another side to our personality—the shadow.

At nearly the same time as the depth psychology of Freud and Jung emerged, a number of writers were producing stories depicting rather strange experiences— tales of characters not being themselves, entering states more frightening than so-called mental illness. These stories concerned individuals confronting a kind of specter, a phantom of themselves in the outer world—the phenomenon of the double. There are many cases of the double in literature from the middle to late nineteenth century—from Oscar Wilde, Guy de Maupassant, E. T. A. Hoffmann, Dostoevsky, and Mary Shelley, to name but a few. Such examples of the double in literature are examined by the psychoanalyst Otto Rank, a contemporary of Freud, in his monograph *The Double*.[1] As it happens, literature and film have done a far better job depicting this phenomenon than psychology. The genre seems to have faded, and, with its demise, our understanding of how fear can usurp our humanness has dwindled as well. We are left with standard psychological categories, which attribute the loss of authenticity to psychological difficulties.

While the double takes many different forms, it usually contains aspects of one's self-image but is perceived as having a will of its own. Guy de Maupassant's story "The Horla," for example, portrays a double with a ghost-like quality, but a ghost bent on giving more than a momentary scare.[2] It saps the very life force out of the main character of the story, who remains unnamed. The appearance of the double occurs quite suddenly:

> A year ago last autumn, I suddenly began having strange, inexplicable fits of uneasiness. At first it was a kind of nervous anxiety that kept me awake for whole nights, in such a state of tension that the slightest sound made me start. I became ill-tempered. I often flew into a rage for no reason. I called in a doctor. He prescribed potassium bromide and showers.

As the narrator tells his story to an assembled group of doctors and scientists, he relates the many mysterious things that have happened to him. A decanter of water at his bedside, filled before sleep, was empty every morning. He eventually contrives a test to make sure that he himself has not drunk the water during the night. He describes seeing a rose breaking off from a bush one day and rising in the air, as if taken up to be smelled by an invisible being. He tells of feeling a presence in his room while he was reading, as if someone were looking over his shoulder. When he turned, a mirror on the other side of the room no longer reflected his image. After a few moments his image reappeared, as if something standing between him and the mirror had moved out of the way.

At the end of the session with the doctors and researchers, the narrator tells who he thinks this invisible presence may be:

So you see, gentlemen, a Being, a new Being which will no doubt multiply as we have done, has just appeared on earth. . . . What is it? Gentlemen, it's the being the earth has been awaiting, after man! He's come to dethrone us, subjugate us, tame us, perhaps feed on us, as we feed on cattle and hogs. We've always had a foreboding of him, for centuries we've dreaded him and announced his coming. . . . And in everything that you yourselves have been doing for years, gentlemen, in what you call hypnotism, suggestion, animal magnetism, you've been announcing him for years. . . . I tell you that he has come. He's prowling the earth, hesitant as the first men were, still not knowing the extent of his strength and power, though he'll know it soon, too soon.

The appearance of the double in literature at the same time as depth psychology's emergence suggests that artists and psychologists were getting at similar phenomena from different points of view; they were both concerned with how we lose the sense of ourselves. Psychologists determined that all such phenomena originated within the psyche of the individual as a result of one's personal life history. Otto Rank, for example, explicitly reduces the artistic presentation of the double to personal difficulties experienced by the writers of such stories. He described de Maupassant as being the product of a hysterical mother, and as also having a predisposition toward mental illness, a speculation backed up by the fact that de Maupassant's younger brother suffered from hysterical paralysis. Other writers who portray the double are similarly diagnosed by Rank. He lays the origin of the tales of E. T. A. Hoffmann at the feet of yet another hysterical mother. He ascribes the strange double tales of Poe, such as "William Wilson," to alcohol. He accounts for Dostoevsky's fascination with the double as stemming from his epilepsy. Psychology subsumed the problem of the double into nothing more than a symptom of mental derangement. It became one of the signs of psychosis, paranoia, or an indication of excessive egocentric tendencies. The double was reduced to an hallucinatory experience rather than a cultural reality.

Rank's interpretation was understandable, given that in many cases the appearance of the double in literature paralleled the life of the writers. One such incident is reported by Goethe, in his autobiography, *Fiction and Truth*. Goethe says:

> Then one of the strangest premonitions came over me. I saw myself—not with my real eyes, but those of my mind—riding on horseback toward me on the same road and clothed in a garment such as I had never worn: its color was the gray of a pike, with some gold in it. As soon as I roused myself from this dream, the figure completely disappeared. It is strange, however, that after eight years I found myself on this same road, going to visit Friederike once more, wearing the garment of which I had dreamed and which I was wearing not from choice but by accident.

The double often appears as someone who looks exactly like oneself, but the experience has many variations. In de Maupassant's story, the presence did not reveal itself in quite this form. It did, however, drink the water belonging to the narrator and seemed to be reading his books, looking over his shoulder, doing all the things that the narrator himself did. In most of these nineteenth-century stories, the double presents itself as externalized. Goethe's account offers a twist, in that he saw the double figure, not physically but *as if* physically, with the mind's eye. In Goethe's description, he found himself on the same road he'd traveled earlier, now dressed as the apparition that had appeared to him eight years earlier. The psychical appearance of the double always seems to have actual physical results. His recognition that the double appears through the mind's eye rather than the physical eye suggests that Goethe was much more alert and aware than others who had such experiences. His powers of observation were more astute, probably stemming from his work as a scientific researcher as well as a poet. If one does not have such capacities, image and perceptual reality easily become confused. This detail is important because it suggests that full alertness is required to detect when we are affected by the double.

To explore the phenomenon of the double we have to free ourselves from the bias of psychological explanations. Rank, for example, understood the double as a manifestation of narcissism. When the ego is threatened with dissolution, either by impending death or the loss of love, it preserves itself by producing an external image of itself. That is the typical psychological explanation of the double.

Rather than viewing the artists who introduced the double as psychologically demented, I prefer to look on them as prophets. Surely Dostoevsky, Goethe,

Hoffmann, Poe, Stevenson, Shelley, Wilde, Stoker, and Baudelaire were expressing something deeper and more meaningful than their own problems with Mom. What these artists prophetically imagined was intuitive perception in the form of images—images not of their own supposedly deranged psyches but of the future, of where humanity was heading.

When the narrator in de Maupassant's story says that something is coming to overtake humanity, he also presents an image of it. At the very end of the story, he says that he intuitively feels that the arrival of the double has something to do with a Brazilian ship he saw sailing into port as he looked out from his house overlooking the Seine. He speculates that the ghostly being arriving on the ship is connected to a curse that has ravaged an area of Brazil, citing an account he read in the newspaper:

> A kind of epidemic of madness seems to have been raging for some time in the state of São Paulo. The inhabitants of several villages have fled, abandoning their fields and houses, claiming to have been pursued and eaten by invisible vampires that fed on their breath while they were asleep, and drank nothing but water and milk.

The narrator suggests that the ghost found its way onto the Brazilian freighter, but the reader is meant to associate it with the ruthless destruction of the Brazilian landscape. The ship was filled with cargo extracted from the natural resources around the villages, and de Maupassant paints a picture of exploitative commercialism, of lands ravaged to satisfy the material desires of the world. It is as if cutting the trees, clearing the land, extracting the minerals left no places for this strange being to hide.

The picture presented by this suffering individual—a world completely at the mercy of materialistic desires, and technology—has now arrived at our port. In this world, we no longer see the whole of the world but only ourselves, and then only a vastly reduced image of ourselves. We see our materialistic greed and feel separate from the beyond, but this separation is our own doing. When we now imagine the world, it is a double world, not the fullness and the plenitude of the soul world together with the earthly world, the great union of the visible and the invisible.

The division of worlds maintains itself through the presence of fear. We would feel the pain of losing the fullness of existence much more acutely were it not for a fear and the agent it uses to make us forgetful of what we have lost, the double. While psychological interpretations reduce the double to a problem of narcissism, the literary authors were not caught in egotism. Rather, they perceived the double, an eager, covetous, conceited, envious, egoistic force within the world, an autonomous force that often adopts our human image in its quest for world domination.

Rather than trying to identify the force that lies behind the double, which would take us into matters of theology, it is perhaps more useful to set about the task of describing how it functions, and the different forms it takes. The ways in which the double makes us forgetful of our humanity have been set forth in the previous chapters: fears multiply in the world, constrict the body, enter with great strength into consciousness, and we begin to function as something other than ourselves. While the authors cited above imagined the double as an external figure, it has now entered into our very being, where its function is to keep us numb from the overwhelming presence of fear. In this manner, fears are allowed to increase in the world, relatively free of opposition.

The Individual Double

We can be present to the most horrendous atrocities in the world and yet the depth of the tragedy does not penetrate to the core of our soul. We can even wonder how it is that we can be so unfeeling, so unresponsive. Are we really ourselves, or have we become a double of ourselves? A double has no soul; it looks and acts human, seems to others to be human, but is no more than a kind of automaton. If we find ourselves unresponsive to the presence of suffering in the world and are instead occupied with our own comfort, perhaps this is due to the influence of doubling. We can see on television the results of a devastating earthquake that has killed thousands of people, and proceed with our lives, only momentarily shaken. We can drive by the worst slums of the city every day on the way to work, and the suffering leaves little lasting impression. One must conclude that, in our souls, we have lost touch with ourselves.

Even today, the double sometimes appears as an external image. We have all had experiences of feeling that someone is standing directly behind us or that someone we know is nearby. Or we may find ourselves feeling as though we are again in a place we know we have never been in before, so-called déjà vu experiences. We may also hear our name called, and turn to see no one we know. In 1917, Rudolf Steiner said that children in the future would more and more find themselves accompanied by an invisible companion who would urge them to do destructive things, and he was not speaking of imaginary playmates.

The individual double can appear during drug states, or it may be initiated by excessive loneliness, isolation, or an incapacity to love. It may also appear in dreams as an image of oneself, usually possessing unsavory characteristics, something quite different from what Jung termed the shadow, and also different from merely seeing oneself as one of the dream figures.

The narrator in de Maupassant's story says to the doctors that hypnosis experiments have been preparing for the appearance of the double. Indeed, the individual double figures centrally in hypnosis, past-life regression, and shamanic journeying, all of which rely on the induction of a trance state. Whenever we are not fully conscious, there is an opportunity for the double to come in and take hold of us. When, for example, one goes on a shamanic journey, the trip usually begins with rhythmic drumming, and then one is instructed to go to an inner landscape and meet some kind of magical figure—an animal, a fairy, elf, gnome, or healer. The person who goes to this landscape is not ourselves, however. We are sitting in the room, consciousness lowered, in a trance state. It is the double who takes this journey for us.

I have asked numerous people who engage in shamanic work the question of who goes on the journey, and none has given a clear answer. Most of them say that it is part of the soul. But it must be something much closer to the ego, for the being that goes on the journey is a reflection of ourselves. The double apparently has the capacity to voyage between worlds, and perhaps even the capacity to go to other times. A current popularizing of hypnotism, past-life regression, and shamanic practices looks on any altered state of consciousness as something helpful. When consciousness is altered, however, caution needs to be taken in giving ourselves over to what appears to be an enlargement of consciousness but in fact may be a doubling of ourselves.

A person who employs any kind of hypnotic technique risks binding the spirit of the one hypnotized. This binding is evident, showing itself as the relinquishing of body and consciousness to the hypnotist, and the peculiar things the hypnotized subject may do under the power of suggestion. We simply have to ask, who does these things? The hypnotist suggests them, and it looks as if the hypnotized person carries them out, but the person is not really there. The individual spirit can become bound to the double. If people assent to such a diminishing of their consciousness, their agreement does not make it a free act. They have merely agreed to relinquish freedom. Any benefits that might result from such practices are quite secondary to what has been lost. The bound spirit will lose some of the creative capacity needed to confront the circumstances of daily life. Even temporary benefits do not outweigh the gravity of a diminished spirit.

The wish for powers beyond the range of ordinary consciousness can be no more than a distraction from the task of confronting fear. Going inward by using these now popular trance techniques can become a form of running away. It must be said that the popularizing of trance states deviates considerably from the depth of tradition characteristic of true shamanic practices. Weekend shamanism has little to do with the knowledge and wisdom developed in cultures over centuries. In such cultures, shamanism is a vocation, a calling requiring years and years of training, and exists always within a community, a culture, and a religious worldview.

We need not be directly hypnotized to find ourselves overtaken by the individual double. If I become extremely angry, there may come a moment in the anger when I distinctly recognize that some other consciousness has taken over. It is even possible, while angry, to become a passive witness, to look at the enraged person who looks exactly like me and realize that he is not me. Or I may go shopping, look into a window, and see something very expensive that I would like to own. I can be standing there, again, witnessing the one who has now become completely captured by the item desired, and watch that person go in and use a credit card to buy what I cannot afford. The whole campaign for advertising the item, which I may well have seen on television and not remember, has lulled me into a kind of trance, giving the double to opportunity to enter.

The character of the individual double is inexorably

linked with the way fear is brought into the world. Robert Jay Lifton, in his study of the Nazi doctors who performed atrocious experiments on human beings, came to the conclusion that these diabolical researchers were able to enact such horrors because of the process of doubling.[3] According to Lifton's research, doubling has recognizable characteristics. The doctors saw themselves as humane physicians, husbands, and fathers. At the same time, they saw themselves as performing these atrocities quite freely, without being coerced. This duality shows us that the double can function alongside what we consider to be our normal selves without any recognizable conflict.

Lifton details five characteristics of the doubling process: (1) A second self forms autonomously alongside the ordinary self. (2) The second self comes about as a direct result of living in an ongoing state of fear. (3) The second self gives coherence to living with ongoing fear. It makes such a situation seem normal. (4) The second self performs unacceptable and atrocious acts. (5) Conscience is transferred from the ordinary self to this second self.

The duality of doubling is different from the sort of cognitive dissociation that I've identified as numbness. The terror inflicted by the Nazis did not require the numbing of the healthy, functioning self. The double came to speak for the entire self, without any realization that this replacement had happened. What prompted the doubling was the fear that the doctors themselves lived within. They lived daily with the threat of their own extinction if they did not carry out the orders given. The harm done to others was seen as a matter of duty, as loyalty to the group. The doctors thus did not feel any responsibility or guilt for their outrageous acts. Without realizing it, their moral consciousness had radically changed.

In describing the process of doubling, Lifton is in no way pardoning the actions of the doctors or suggesting they were not responsible for their actions. Once we become aware of the double, a new dimension of responsibility opens. We now must be responsible not just for what we do, but for the condition of our moral consciousness. Attributing doubling to extraordinary evil or to some kind of possession and not as a part of everyday existence sidetracks us from the work we must do to retain soul life.

The doubling undergone by the doctors took place within an institutional structure that encouraged and even demanded it. There is evidence that Adolf Hitler engaged in certain occult rituals involving trance states of consciousness. Hitler was a diminutive man, but something took hold of him when he stood up to address the masses, and he was able to induce in his audience a shift in their moral consciousness. Later, to maintain his own state of doubling, he took ever increasing quantities of drugs. Out of this, he was able to create an institutional structure of fear, National Socialism. Of this institution Hitler said: "Those who see in National Socialism nothing more than a political movement know scarcely anything of it. It is more even than a religion. It is the will to create mankind anew."

Hitler's only boyhood friend, August Kubizek, was present when his double first appeared. Hitler was seventeen at the time, and it was after a performance of Wagner's *Rienzi*. Kubizek said:

> It was as if another being spoke out of his body, and moved him as much as it did me. It wasn't at all a case of a speaker being carried away by his own words. On the contrary; I rather felt as though he himself listened with astonishment and emotion to what burst forth from him with elementary force . . . it was a state of complete ecstasy and rapture. . . . He spoke of a special mission which one day would be entrusted to him.

Today, as we look back at the Holocaust, we may feel secure that as long as we keep this tragedy within our collective memory it cannot be repeated. Such an attitude is completely naïve. The more that fear intensifies in the world, the greater the possibility that just such a wide-scale doubling will occur without our recognition of it.

Institutional Doubles

The process of doubling has nothing to do with dissociation, multiple-personality states, or what today in psychology are diagnosed as borderline states. The potential for losing the sense of who we are exists for anyone living with an overwhelming presence of fear. To live with only those capacities of consciousness that understand material reality, to have no capability of conscious soul or spirit life, or to seek such experiences in unhealthy ways opens the gateway for the entrance of the double. A culture such as our own, then, that focuses so much on materialistic values, is ripe to have its basic institutional structures invaded by the double.

For an example of how an institution becomes suffused with the double, we can look at science. Scientific discoveries that are rapidly incorporated into the larger culture are often associated with a sudden breakthrough on the part of researchers. A recent example can be found in the individual who discovered gene coding. This individual worked for many years on the problem. Then, one day, as he was driving to work on a freeway in California, thinking about his work, he was lulled into a kind of trance state by the repetitious activity of freeway driving and traffic. All of sudden, the answer to the problem of genetic coding came to him. His solution turned out to be correct, and within a short time the technical means to utilize "genetic fingerprinting" was developed. This technology is now widely used for determining whether someone accused of crimes such as rape or murder is guilty. If blood or semen is available, its genetic code can be matched with that of the accused. Interestingly, this researcher regrets that his discovery was taken up so readily by the scientific community, because of the other possible misuses his research could lead to.

The history of science is replete with such stories. We tend to look at them as paradigmatic of scientific creativity and discovery, even though they often proceed without a conscious understanding of their effects on soul life. Some scientific discoveries involve individuals who have developed an imaginative capacity of consciousness. An individual such as David Bohm, for example, who made significant discoveries in physics, had a well-developed imaginative worldview. His discoveries came out of a life dedicated to developing the capacity to perceive an individual event in the context of wholeness. Quick discoveries often do not have this background, and the possibility of these discoveries coming, not from a fully developed imagination but as a kind of dark gift from a double, is strong.

Imaginative science has to be distinguished from technical science. The former proceeds in the light of imaginal cognition, while the latter puts faith in the use of the scientific method as the road to discovery. The latter often produces results that look beneficial at the outset but eventually turn out to be destructive. DDT seemed an answer to prevent diseases transmitted by insects; years later it was found to be a cancer-causing agent. How many drugs that seem to be helpful are producing long-range harm? Technological innovations often follow a similar pattern. The Internet, for example, seems to be a revolutionary technical achievement. No one thus far, however, has developed the imagination to look at it in terms of its impact on soul life. While the Internet is touted as the greatest tool of communication since printing, it may well be a kind of double of communication. Look at how much is erased by relating in cyberspace. The body is excluded, the nuances of speaking eliminated, the importance of what is left unsaid, gone. E-mail, for example, is not at all like writing a letter. E-mailing is typically done in haste. We expect an immediate answer. Communication has more or less been reduced to the transfer of information.

The difficulty with technical science in which innovation is not guided by soul consciousness is that doing gets ahead of knowing. The gaps in our knowledge are the primary way in which the double becomes incorporated into institutional life, whether this is the institutional life of science, economics, education, or any other field.

The double finds entry into cultural and institutional life particularly through disciplines in which our humanity is central. Many of these disciplines have adopted the scientific method without having any notion of the kind of reality they are dealing with. In the nineteenth century, psychology, sociology, economics, and politics took the scientific method and applied it directly to human beings, as if elements crucial to this level of reality—like soul, spirit, freedom, will—could be objectified and quantified. Behavioral psychology conceives of human beings in terms of the more elemental aspects of behavior, and then advertising uses this understanding to manipulate us. Modern economic theory lies behind the manipulation of interest rates and is based on a view of the human being as centered in self-interests. Politics uses the instruments of polls rather than an understanding of the good to determine public policy. All of these pave the way for the entrance of the double.

Once a double of the cultural world becomes entrenched, even when the difficulties become apparent, an attempt to remedy the situation will partake of the same kind of consciousness that produced the difficulties in the first place. Since the fact that we live in a double world remains hidden to us, it couldn't be otherwise. The only possible resolution then becomes a complete break-down of the institution in which the double has taken up residence. It's as if our collective soul has been sealed inside a Chinese puzzle box, and our only chance of free-dom is to smash the box. Such an entrenchment is the double's way of keeping us in a state of ongoing fear. We seem to have no choice but to wait for total collapse, which introduces more fear and the need to hold even more tightly to illusion. One shouldn't underestimate the cleverness of the double. It will always use fear to create ever more clever variations of itself.

Becoming Aware of Doubles

The task of becoming aware of when we are not fully our-selves can be daunting. If there are times when we are not acting like ourselves, we think that there must be some-thing psychologically wrong with us. We further believe that such problems can be fixed by therapy or drug inter-vention. The problem of doubling, however, is not just a problem of individual psychology but a problem of living within a culture of fear.

The first step to becoming alert to the possibility of

doubling is to guard against anything that diminishes our consciousness. Unfortunately, the things that diminish consciousness are often put forward as doing exactly the opposite. Besides hypnotism and shamanic practices already mentioned, there are many movements offering consciousness expansion that actually diminish consciousness. Neurolinguistic programming, motivation techniques making it possible to walk over hot coals, EST, transcendental meditation, meditation tapes, and many New Age practices need to be approached with a great deal of caution. Even some psychotherapies can make one subject to the powers of suggestion, as instances of false-memory syndrome seem to indicate. The fact that these practices intend to be helpful to others does not alter the fact that they call for a handing over of the most delicate and precious part of ourselves to others, often to people who have no idea of what they are dealing with.

In daily life, it is possible to catch the operation of the double out of the corner of the eye. Moments in which we become aware that our consciousness has been captured by television, computers, advertising, journalism, or political jargon can stop the double at the doorway. In this domain, cognition becomes all important, but not just ordinary cognition. The heart cannot be invaded by the double, so development of its soul capacities becomes a central protection. Intuitive perception cannot be deceived. This capacity cannot be given to us by others; it has to be developed solely out of inner freedom and ongoing research into one's own consciousness. One aspect of consciousness of particular value as a protection against unwittingly losing a sense of ourselves is conscience. Conscience forms the greatest protector against doubles.

The traditional understanding of conscience as an inner voice that warns us when something may be about to lead us astray has to be reviewed in light of the strength of fear in the world and the intrusion of doubling into conscious life. We cannot experience conscience unless we recognize consciousness as a full-body phenomena. We have to be able to feel when, in the presence of fear, it comes to us that we can sidestep fear by yielding to something that seems to be us but is not. Our body ought to cringe at the possibility of being something not quite fully human.

A first step toward the awakening of conscience can be made by reviewing the course of our actions at the end of each day. It is important not only to think about what we have done but also to picture the unfolding of the events of the day and our encounters with others. We can go even further and imagine the effects of our actions on the lives of others, to try to picture what happens to other people in concrete ways. We should not sit in judgment of ourselves, but just observe our actions impartially. Such a practice can help restore the inner voice of conscience, yet it is not enough. The more numb our body, the harder it is to alter our actions, even as we become more aware of their effects in the world. We also have to work toward awakening inner, bodily awareness.

Our body will begin to awaken if we do more than look at everything we see—plants, hills, animals, houses, other people—in physical form and make an inner task of observing how all that surrounds us is interwoven. We can focus on the dynamic interplay of things in the world rather than directly on the things themselves. Look at the overlapping of clouds, at rising mists, how light breaks through, how landscape hardens in cold and widens in warmth, how contours form and disappear. If you make this a practice, very distinct feelings will arise: a sadness combined, paradoxically, with joy. Who has not felt this quality when watching the orange glow of the sunset and the moment-to-moment change of the color of the clouds, now glowing with the light of gold, then passing into orange, then shades of purple, and gradually fading over into gray? Not only do we experience feelings of awe in the presence of such beauty, we also feel a little sad.

In becoming present to the rhythms of the world, we become sensitive to what is behind these revelations, something lawful that connects everything coming into being and passing away. The illusion that we are bound to ourselves, trapped in our body, perhaps even trapped in the head begins to dissolve. We too are part of the larger world process, coming into birth and dying away, not just at the beginning and end of our lives, but as a constant process going on from moment to moment. Experiencing ourselves as part of this ongoing rhythm of the world can help strip away our vanity.

A new sense of conscience arises from immersing ourselves in the subtle interweavings of world processes, of which we are a part. Anyone who has spent time with the natural world in these ways cannot come away from the experience without wondering deeply about the significance of their life, without looking at what they are doing and perhaps how far away they have gotten from what is really important. The urge we often feel to get away from it all, to go on a trip, to spend time in the wilderness, comes not only as an imagined relief from the stress of everyday life but also as a healthy warning signal that we may be on the way to losing ourselves. The soul prompts us to retrieve what we are losing.

The poet Novalis, in his novel *Heinrich von Ofterdingen*, approaches the question of conscience in this new way.[4] The particular passage occurs as a conversation between Henry and a pilgrim, Sylvester:

"When will the time come," asks Henry, "when all fear, all pain, all need and all evil is removed from the universe?"

"When there is only one power—the power of conscience. When nature has become chaste and moral. There is only one cause for evil—common weakness; and this weakness is nothing else than limited moral receptiveness; and lack of interest in freedom."

"Please help me to understand the nature of conscience."

"If I could do that, I would be God, for conscience arises in the act of understanding it."

When Sylvester says that all fear will be removed from the universe when nature becomes chaste and moral, he includes human beings in the rhythms of nature. We may not be able to see it, but our actions, when influenced by the double, not only harm ourselves and others but also diminish the life of nature. Does not the world seem to be just a little bit more frozen when we have acted out of anger, hate, envy, or fear? Feeling the touch of sadness upon experiencing nature's rhythms is a way of realizing how out of touch we have become with the whole. Our moral receptivity weakens the more we separate ourselves from the rhythms of the world. Sylvester makes an interesting observation—that weakness also arises from a lack of interest in freedom. Freedom usually means to be free from external constraints, to be free to *do* something. This usual sense of the word, though, has nothing to do with the essence of human freedom, which lies in each of us being exactly who we are, not just in an external way but in soul and spirit as well.

While conscience is awakened by our body in its participation in world rhythms, it also arises from an inner feeling for the results of our actions. This realm of feeling is different from ordinary feelings of guilt. Guilt feelings stem from moral precepts that have been instilled in us by others—parents, education, religion. When we act in ways contrary to the moral codes that have been instilled, we feel guilt. The moral situations we now encounter have become far more complicated than our outmoded moral codes can handle, however, and guilt no longer serves as an effective guide. In addition, we are much more aware of how moral codes have been used in ways they were not meant to be. Millions of people have been coerced because so-called moral authorities have used their power to instill feelings of guilt. A new realm of moral feeling must arise, an inner feeling centered in the heart, of belonging to or deviating from the dynamic order of the forces that weave together the world.

If I become sensitive in a bodily way to natural world rhythms, I can quite distinctly feel when I am not acting in accordance with soul and spirit qualities in life. In that moment I may not know the basis of feeling out of harmony, but it brings me nonetheless to reflection. I may then remember specific actions that seemed to announce the presence of the double. Perhaps I remember shouting at my partner, and now, rather than taking it as just a moment of irritability, I can see that it was not quite myself who spoke in anger. I am not thereby relieved of the responsibility for that act—I cannot palm it off on my double. Indeed, my responsibility increases, for I feel more acutely the importance of being present and aware of what I am doing and not simply acting impulsively. With this heightening of consciousness, I am forging a new sense of conscience.

To become bodily present to world rhythms as a way of awakening a new sense of conscience would seem to throw us right into the cauldron of fear. As described earlier, the natural world, too, is pervaded by fear. We are indeed approaching a time when the natural rhythms of the world will have become so disturbed that this means for awakening consciousness may no longer be available. The sun still rises and sets, clouds still form and dissolve, plants still grow, and animals roam. But, there can be no doubt, fear is also present. This means that simply enjoying the qualities of the natural world cannot in themselves awaken conscience in the manner described. A more reciprocal relation with the rhythms of the natural world must be established. We cannot turn to nature only for our own enjoyment and refreshment and regeneration. Our participation with nature must become a practice, consciously oriented toward coming to a right relation with our body. Under these circumstances, we can seek the grounding of moral consciousness needed for our time, and the fear present in the natural world cannot dominate.

CHAPTER 7

———

Love Casts Out Fear

We have been looking at ways to work on our imaginative life so that the forces necessary for soul life can become conscious and balance the presence of fears. Another force necessary to counter fear is love. Imagination and love go together. Without love, imagination easily becomes a mental trick. All of the exercises in this book require centering imagination in the region of the heart and not the head alone. This centering assures that soul develops in tandem with love. Without imagination, however, love easily becomes confused sentimentality.

Love and fear form the great opposites of the world. Love can even transform the Earth into the substance of love. The whole evolution of the Earth and of human beings points in the direction of their fulfillment through this mighty force, the only force that can subdue the ravages of fear. All spiritual traditions, in spite of their many differences, resound with this common theme. The transformation of Earth into a planet of love will not happen by itself. The task lies in the hands of human beings, for we are the instruments through which love circulates.[1]

Fear relies for its survival on our reluctance to submit our feelings to scrutiny. We often prefer the vague sentimentality, the drama, or the sense of mystery that accompanies feelings. We imagine that if we examine our feelings too closely, the drama of our lives might disappear. It is equally possible, however, to enter the mystery of the feeling life and discover more of its subtleties, nuances, and richness. Soul life would thereby be increased rather than diminished. Overcoming our resistance to examining love is a critical step in conquering the presence of fear.

Love does not belong wholly to the human realm. We cannot possess it, control it, or make it do our bidding. Plato, for example, understood love as belonging to a realm between the divine and the human. Love connects us with the gods. Plato has Socrates imagine Eros as a daemon, a go-between, trafficking between the spiritual and the earthly worlds. Further, other kinds of love exist in addition to *eros,* or erotic love. *Philia,* or soul-friendship, also belongs to the daemonic realities of love. The Christian world added *agape,* or selfless love. From the point of view of love as multiple daemonic beings, our task as human beings lies in developing the capacities to be proper vessels through which the forces of love can work.

Eros awakens bodily attraction coupled with imaginative exploration. Philia awakens the feeling of intimacy, the bond of friendship. Agape awakens the feeling of doing something for the sake of another without expectation of compensation. In our time, the differentiated appearance of these forms of love has collapsed, and they seem to us to be no more than intellectual categories. Fear has successfully made a muddle of the capacity to clearly differentiate our feelings.

A rehabilitation of the feeling life begins with re-imagining love. Rather than seeing only the three classical categories, this re-imagination allows us to see that love functions in four distinct modes—sexual love, emotional love, spiritual love, and creative love. These four modes relate closely with the classical modes. We can think of it this way: Eros now manifests in one way as sexual love but manifests in a different way as emotional love. Philia manifests as emotional love but also as spiritual love, and agape manifests as spiritual love but also as creative love.

Sexual Love

Plato's myth of human sexuality, told in the *Symposium,* gives a picture of the original human being as a comfortable creature, round in form, who happily rolled along in the world, quite self-satisfied, having no needs and no aspirations. Zeus became irritated with the complacency of these creatures and split the indulgent spherical beings in two with a lightning bolt. Each half now searches for its other half, expressed in our soul life as sexual desire. Love first shows itself in the human world as the pressing need to unite our body with another body. This need operates indiscriminately. We find ourselves attracted to many different people; this is neither bad nor immoral. Within the boundaries of socialized behavior, this attraction celebrates and proclaims the wonder of our physical existence.

Feeling aroused by the presence of sexual desire does not mean that sex must necessarily follow. The surge of sexual feeling jolts us into an awareness of something affecting our body that, while it registers within the physiology of the body, cannot be reduced to mere physiology. Physiology does not cause these feelings but merely provides the medium through which they function.

If the presence of love announcing itself in a bodily way is denied or suppressed, if it becomes strongly connected with fear or guilt, or if it is understood as something "only physical," have we not turned away from the most basic way that love manifests itself in the world? Love shows itself in a sensory manner as a powerful force, bringing about our most fundamental, strongest, and most immediate connection with others. This connection is far broader than genital sexuality. Perhaps the most powerful deterrent against fear is the feeling of the warmth of bodily connection with others. If we lose this mode of connection, we feel isolated and alone, set up for all the ploys of one kind of fear or another.

If this force of love flowing within the body is approached recklessly, not understood as a sacred presence within the body but only as natural urges demanding satisfaction, have we not then, in a different way, also turned against love's physical presence? Love celebrates its entry into the world through a vivifying presence within the human body where it lives as sexual desire. It does not leave us even in old age. Its rhythm and intensity may vary, but its presence remains constant.

As a society, we are still ambiguous toward sensual love, in a large part due to organized religion. Religion has often been a vehicle for bodily fears by declaring that the blissful presence of sex in the world might detract our attention from the divine. Religion retains its authority by declaring the divine to be completely separate from the physical world. It is not idolatrous, however, to consider the torrent of desire to be holy; indeed, it is our sensuous connection with the divine world. Suppression of our sexual being suppresses love in the world and opens us to the onslaught of fears.

Because we have had to hide our sexuality, both from ourselves and from others, it has withdrawn itself from the center of our being and is homeless. The strong emphasis on things sexual in every sphere of modern life—movies, advertisements, music, and on the streets—does not constitute a sign of its strength, but of its weakness. Because it is misplaced, it thrashes about like something about to die, a force completely out of balance. Few have so clearly recognized how out of balance we are in the sexual sphere as the poet Rainer Maria Rilke:

> Physical pleasure is a sensual experience no different from pure seeing or the pure sensation [with] which a fine fruit fills the tongue; it is a great unending experience, which is given us, a knowing of the world, the fullness and the glory of all knowing. And not our acceptance of it is bad; the bad thing is that most people misuse and squander this experience and apply it as a stimulant at the tired spots of their lives and as distraction instead of rallying toward exalted moments.[2]

Displacing the fullness of our sexual being into the narrowness of genital sexuality only momentarily distracts us from our fears, whereas entering the fullness of our being through desire keeps the divine near. When we feel the full attractiveness of others, we are able to shed the need to be constantly on guard. Love considered in this way does not constitute a panacea. The fires of desire are certainly not comfortable. Rilke, though, reminds us that there is more to sex than internal urgings, and that we needn't feel we ought to have the strength to put those urgings aside to get on with more important religious matters. A full knowing of the world, he suggests, cannot take place if sexual desire is cast aside like something rotten. Without desire, knowledge is filled with mental and intellectual abstractions and is not in touch with the living body of the world. If sex, having been de-centered, then returns forcefully in an unhealthy way as a cultural obsession, it exists side by side with an unhealthy thought life. We become spectators of the world, rather than participants in the heart of reality.

Knowing through desire brings about a new contact with the world, knowing as healing. With this form of intimate knowing we become interested in connections, synthesis, wholeness, and a productive rather than analytic form of contact with others and the world. Novalis is another poet who gave deep consideration to questions of the sensuous body. In his aphorisms, he says:

All absolute sensation is religious.[3]

We must receive the body as the soul in our dominion. The body is the instrument for the formation and modification of the world. We must therefore seek to form our body as a wholly capable organ. Modification of our instrument is the modification of the world.[4]

There is only one temple in the world, and that is the human body. Nothing is holier than this highest form. One touches heaven when one touches a human body.[5]

Living the presence of love within the body in a healthy manner has nothing to do with whether we do or don't engage in the act of sex. Nonetheless, religion has often attempted to remove from us the freedom to struggle with this force in the right way by labeling sex a sin. In this way, religion allowed fear to enter the holy sanctum of sexuality. Sexual desire constitutes a divine force. Its fires form our body into an organ for the modification of the world. As individuals, we are responsible for giving this force a home and allowing it to form us into capable beings.

Because the force of sexual love takes up residence in each individual human body, it is the responsibility of each individual to undergo the rigors of life's instruction concerning how this force wants to shape itself in each individual instance. In this realm, general rules or laws inculcate fear, whether they call for prohibitions or unbridled indulgence.

Learning the particularities of how love inhabits one's body takes a long time. Individuals vary tremendously in the intensity, rhythms, and importance of desire. Finding the right relation to this force is a wholly individual matter, demanding a high degree of inner presence and observation. Such reflection often has to be developed in the midst of a torrent of passion that seems to want only to give itself away. For young people in particular, sex constitutes a beautiful difficulty, filling them with impatience and haste. What a difference it would make if they understood that this difficulty stems from the announcement of the force of love awakening within, if they knew the importance of housing this force carefully.

Sexual desire announces itself in the body before we are fully human beings. We are born into human form, but, along with other significant developments, the fires of desire are required to forge an inner life through which we grow gradually into our humanity. Desire's urgings are unruly, impetuous, frustrating, and demanding. We would be mistaken, however, to think that these urgings seek only their release. Desire lives in the body as a deep reservoir for bringing love into the world. Contain the fire; guard the flame. Let it do its work of purifying the body, making an inner space that prepares for the possibility of a soul life entwined with the glory and perfection of physical life.

Emotional Love

Sexual desire carries a strong impersonal component. We may find ourselves physically attracted without an emotional connection. Conversely, an emotional connection can exist prior to sexual attraction and may continue to exist after it. Emotional love does not derive from sexual love; it has autonomy. It should not be viewed as a higher form of love but simply as another form, existing alongside and sometimes in tandem with other forms of love.

The purpose of sexual love differs from that of emotional love. The former constitutes a current flowing through the body, igniting the fires of transformation that, when tended carefully, make the body into a vessel that can contain not just sexual love, but all forms of love. The latter constitutes a current flowing through the soul, and similarly makes the soul into a vessel of receptivity, inspiring true imagination, a necessity for dealing with fear in healthy ways. Learning to contain emotional love gives us the reflective space necessary for forming an inner life, a conscious soul life. Through emotional love, soul becomes a direct and immediate experience; the other person now lives within our imagination.

The holy force of love works into two souls at the same time. Two people, under the sway of this feeling, say that they are *in* love, and thus bound together. Love as an emotion does not really shuttle back and forth between one individual and another. It encompasses and penetrates both involved at the same time. When one says "I am in love with you," the very language proclaims that love is not the connection between two separated beings but that they are in the cauldron together. This mode of love is of itself beautiful, but to be encompassed in this way can be at the same time extremely painful. The beauty belongs to the love; the pain derives from two related sources. On the one hand, it becomes unbearable to imagine that this beauty might be ephemeral, which it is not; it is changeable, yes, but not ephemeral. On the other hand, we often try to rid ourselves of this terrifying beauty by pushing emotion away because it seems to be a radical threat to our individuality. We feel as if we could completely lose ourselves. We discover here, in a very personal way, that love is much greater than our own individual existence.

Fear surrounds emotional love in several ways. It takes advantage of the potential for pain within love to insert itself as a powerful wedge that can initiate an urge to run from what we want most, which is to experience shared love. Fear can become so powerful that we even deny the presence of emotional love. When love comes we have to make a leap of courage into it. To paraphrase Oscar Wilde, the two greatest difficulties in the world are not getting what you want and getting what you want. This dramatic conflict characterizes the visitation of emotional love. In our fear, we may wake up one morning and have the gravest doubt about the reality of what we feel for another person.

While emotional love is not ephemeral, it indeed changes all the time, calm one day, turbulent the next. Love cannot stay the same forever. It may seem to have completely disappeared, and then one day it reappears like a warm breeze through the window, without warning—provided the window has been kept open. Given its seemingly unstable character, the worst difficulties stem from trying to cling to love. We err in expecting happiness as a consequence of emotional love. No peace can be anticipated from this love. Great flexibility of soul is thus required to remain steady on a turbulent sea.

Emotional fears arising from the past of either individual can bring confusion into what we are feeling. Fears lurk in the memory, waiting to attack the pure emotion of love. The emotion of love can be fully trusted; it is a divine force. If it wavers or falters, we can be sure that this is due to the work of fear. If we can catch the moments when fear invades, we will always see that doubt does not enter the emotion itself, but attacks as we *think* about emotion. Once our thinking gets ahead of our feeling, all can be lost. The emotion of love does not signify anything beyond itself. It does not mean that I am forever bound to the other person. Such a decision requires an act of free choice. Fear steps in by implying that emotional love mandates being together forever.

In emotional love, we feel a desire to merge with the other person, but it is not the intention of this form of love. Its intent is to educate us about our separateness from the other person by forcing us to discover it as a true inner experience. That is the paradox of emotional love; it brings us together so that we may discover our separateness. True separateness is not loneliness. It signifies an inner strength, a getting to know our true humanity, a strengthening of the capacity to face fear. We feel loneliness not because we lack a partner but because we are not at home with ourselves. The emptiness we experience cannot be filled by another person, though at first we feel completed by the other. After a while the former emptiness intensifies, usually forcing us to look within. We cannot feel at home with ourselves until we have developed an inner space. The desire to merge meets a healthy resistance, one that must be listened to.

Fear can easily confuse emotional love at the moment when we begin to discover our own individuality in a relationship. As that consciousness awakens, fear seeks to carry the desire to merge beyond its proper boundary, to make us forget the unbridgeable gap between ourselves and the other person. At this point, there is a danger of giving ourselves away before we are fully formed, like a bouquet of flowers that falls to the ground and scatters. We look for a way out of isolation rather than a way into the sacred individuality of our soul, and a loving respect for the soul of the other person. All that comes from this error is pain and confusion. As emotional love intensifies, fear asserts itself to ward off spiritual love, which would otherwise be able to support and deepen emotional love, as well as bring new tasks and challenges. What cannot be accomplished by emotional love can be achieved in spiritual love, which is the complete intermingling of two spirits without the loss of identity of either. Fear seeks to make this merging premature, to make it occur in the wrong sphere, thereby assuring that the two individuals remain trapped in emotion and never meet in spirit.

The heat of emotional love often intensifies sexual love, and the circular current established between sexual and emotional love can become suffocating. A way through this suffocation lies in the direction, not in the spiritual dimension directly, but rather through allowing emotional love to include the factor of friendship.

A form of love exists that partakes of both emotional and spiritual love. The ancient Greeks called it *philia*. These days, when people have formed a sexual-emotional bond that becomes too troublesome, a typical way to break that bond while trying to spare the feelings of the other person is to say, "Let's just be friends." Unfortunately, this ritual of departure betrays the truth that friendship was never part of the sexual-emotional love. Friendship forms an absolutely necessary link to spiritual love and is the single factor that can prevent the claustrophobic restriction of love to its sexual and emotional manifestations. Another crucial aspect of friendship lies in the fact that it belongs to the public and communal realm, an indication that love belongs with the world and should not be held in privacy.

While emotional love has the intent of encompassing two individuals, and of paradoxically driving them out of the emptiness of their aloneness into the fullness of their separateness, when coupled with friendship it becomes the protector of the separateness of the other person. Rilke says:

> I hold this to be the highest task of a bond between two people; that each should stand guard over the solitude of

the other. For, if it lies in the nature of indifference and of the crowd to recognize no solitude, then love and friendship are for the purpose of continually providing the opportunity for solitude. And only those are the true sharings which rhythmically interrupt periods of deep isolation.[6]

Two people cannot serve each other's soul when they are enmeshed and thus engaged in self-serving behavior without realizing it. To disrespect the solitude of another, to fail to be its guardian, not only harms the relationship, it brings harm to the world by preventing the love that has visited the two people from going beyond them into the wider world.

While each mode of love exists autonomously, no mode of love can be bypassed without harm. There are important connections between the modes of love, although these connections are not hierarchical—it is not a matter of rising gradually from a lower state of love to a higher state. The imagination of hierarchy is one of the tricks of fear, where it hides under the guise of power and authority, filling us with the notion that, for example, spiritual love is something higher than sexual love. Spiritual love is different from sexual love, not higher. If we hold it to be something higher, then it is likely that sexual love will be repressed. At the same time, the feeling that we will not achieve the higher forms of love fills us with fear. Being fully present to sexual love, emotional love, and spiritual love at the same time is not in the least bit contradictory. In fact, it is the surest way to free the soul from fear.

Spiritual Love

Fear has worked long and hard to confuse our understanding of spirit in relation to the human being. We see the visible world through our eyes, hear it resound through our ears, come up against it through touch, and receive it through all our senses working in accord. But what surrounds us consists of more than meets the eyes, the ears, the skin. Apart from perceptual qualities, such as lightness and darkness, resonance, and depth, other invisible qualities strike us, such as warmth or coldness of feeling, an imaginative life, thinking, willing. These qualities cannot be apprehended through the senses. The soul is the organ through which we experience such qualities, both in others and in ourselves.

The things and life and qualities around us are not isolated, but interweave with each other. Light weaves into darkness to give us color; the clouds and the sky interweave with the earth; animal life is completely interwoven with the landscape within which it exists; different soul qualities such as imagining, feeling, and thinking interweave with each other. This interweaving takes precedence over the appearance of any single quality; it is responsible for the shape and context of the quality. In the case of human beings, there is also the quality of individuality, which cannot be accounted for by sense perception or experienced through the soul alone. We experience something of the true individuality of another person, not by sensing but through our spirit. Every person is entirely incomparable—matchless, unrivaled, like no other. This defining quality can only be known when our spirit apprehends the spirit of the other.

Spiritual love can be described as a love oriented toward the utterly real but quite invisible aspects of being. It is what allows us to love the innermost mysterious aspects of another person. It goes beyond physical attractiveness, and even qualities of soul, and seeks whatever makes that person completely unique from any other person that has lived or ever will live.

To become conscious of spiritual love requires self-knowledge. The term *self-knowledge* does not mean exactly what it seems. This ancient and honored concept comes to us from the Greeks and is recorded on the temple of Apollo at Delphi: "Know thyself." That inscription has been translated as "Seek self-knowledge," but the word *self* is equivalent to "spirit." We cannot really know our spirit, but we can develop the capacity to know *through* spirit, which is entirely different from intellectual knowledge. Thus, the self-knowledge required for spiritual love means to know through the capacities of spirit. In doing so, one's spirit becomes active and realized, a way of knowing through direct presence.

Knowing through the spirit and spiritual love are exactly the same thing. There can be no difference because what the spirit does is love; the nature of spirit is the nature of love. Finally, no matter what else we may do, fears can only be adequately met and stopped through spiritual love.

In order to experience spiritual love toward another person, one must have a modicum of maturity in the realms of sexual and emotional love. We need to have become proper vessels of love in a bodily way, neither repressing sexual love nor haphazardly spending it for our pleasure alone. And we also need to have matured somewhat in soul life, capable of holding the emotion of love and letting it deepen into the formation of an inner life. To the extent that we have not struggled with and come to recognize the different forms of love, have not felt how they are each autonomous and yet interweave with each other, fear finds its way into the gaps between the modes of love. I may become fearful that sexual love lacks an emotional component, or that emotional love can't seem to come together with sexual desire. Sexual love may seem to bear no connection to spiritual love. I may be confined to one mode of love, fearful of losing that mode in order to explore the ways of the other modes. A constant yielding to love in all its forms is needed to keep the soul free from overwhelming fear.

Spiritual love orients us toward opening to the mystery of another person. This love wants nothing more than to approach the other person in such a manner that spirit shines forth brighter and brighter. Novalis says, "Our spirit is a connecting link to the wholly incomparable."

It is through our own incomparability that we perceive the incomparability of the other and our shared uniqueness. Novalis also says in another aphorism, "I am you." "I am you" does not mean that I find myself in you, which would be a terrible distortion of you as another person. If I find myself in you, and you decide to leave me, then I lose all sense of myself as a human being. This dependency is different from emotional or physical dependency. In emotional dependency, I rely on another person to experience emotion and the semblance of a soul life. In physical dependency, I rely on sexual experience with another to experience my own sexual being. A far graver difficulty arises when, having no sense of my spiritual existence, I rely on the spirit of another: I am effectively dead once the other is no longer in my life.

In spiritual love, the good of the other person lives within every thought that comes to me, whether the thought has to do with the person or not. The spiritual term for this quality is *intent*, which carries a far more subtle meaning than when we say that we intend to do something. Intent carries the sense that something held in thought has become so real as to be literally present—not present before me but everywhere within me. In spiritual love, what becomes so utterly real is the spirit quality of the other person, experienced in the intent to be oriented solely toward the good of the other person.

In daily life, the cultivation of spiritual love centers in the thoughts we bear concerning the other person. These thoughts are not the same as those that emerge from missing someone, from remembering something about our being together in the past, or from thinking about what the person may be doing at the moment. In spiritual love, we do not necessarily think about the other person; rather the other person, as spirit, has become completely interwoven with my existence, so that without even realizing it, he or she is with me every moment, in a way that enhances my own individual freedom rather than hindering it. I locate this quality in the domain of thinking because in ordinary life thinking expresses the life of spirit. This doesn't mean that the content of what we think is necessarily spiritual. The power of thinking itself is a spiritual power, and with spiritual love the spirit of the other person dwells within that power.

If I call someone I love and say that I am thinking about her, this kind of thinking has an emotional intent—it makes someone who is absent present. This is fine and good; it can help keep me in connection with emotion. But that is not spiritual love. In spiritual love, I am every moment concerned with the well-being of the spirit of the other person; it thinks itself within me, pervades my existence completely, and yet leaves me in complete freedom. This kind of love nourishes the soul as well as the spirit of the other person. He or she becomes more of who they are, not more of who we would like them to be.

Spiritual love does not have the rhythmic periodicity characteristic of both sexual love and emotional love. It does not come in waves but is ever-present, reflecting back into the emotions and into the body, giving new coloring and vibrancy to life. Such reflection can also be confusing, allowing us to mistake spiritual love for either sexual or emotional love, both of which are enhanced rather than diminished by spiritual love. We are always being nourished by the spirit, whether through the world around us or through our connections with others. To the extent we are not conscious of this happening, however, we may become tied to sexual and emotional love exclusively, not realizing what form of love is contributing to their enhancement.

As a way of getting to the nature of spiritual knowing and loving, we can contemplate this observation by Novalis:

> Whatever one loves, one finds everywhere, and everywhere sees resemblances and analogies to it. The greater one's love, the vaster and more meaningful is this analogous world. My beloved is the abbreviation of the universe, the universe an elongation, an extrapolation of my beloved. The knowledgeable friend offers all flowers and gifts to his beloved.[7]

When we are touched by spiritual love our whole presence in the world changes. Why do you bring gifts to your beloved? It may be to show your love, but if we are at all thoughtful about what we bring, it comes to more than a demonstration of warmth of feeling. We search and look for just the right thing that expresses something of what we see of that person, of the deepest level of that person, not just what he or she may like and thus feel flattered by. Those who bring worn-out clichés express only their self-centered emotion.

If we bring flowers, they must be exactly the right flowers. If we write a poem, it must picture the world in its analogy to our beloved. And, beyond the bringing of such meaningful gifts, what we do every day, how we get up in the morning, how we approach our work, how we see what is going on in the world—all of this changes. You may find yourself thinking much more imaginatively. Such ways of thinking, far from distorting what we may be thinking about, give us our only true pictures of the world. The world, in every aspect, cannot really be seen except through the eyes of love. We can really know the world only through love.

We can be sure that our love for another has touched the spiritual level when our interest in the world becomes more acute, more vivid, more imaginative. We may find that doing things the way we are accustomed to no longer satisfies; a lack or an emptiness accompanies us. We may find that the work we do, if it has no spiritual meaning, no longer satisfies us. Those relationships lacking in spiritual depth are likely to drop away. Spending leisure time frivolously begins to seem foolish. Instead of deciding a change is needed in life, perhaps it would be more fruitful to sense that a change has already taken place, and begin trying to look at what we are doing through different eyes. If we do not make such an effort, we feel more and more exhausted by continuing on in the same way, and yet cannot really imagine what we could otherwise be doing.

We can begin that effort by acknowledging the deep

significance the experience of love has for us. We have perhaps come to take it for granted, particularly if the romantic phase has passed. The ending of this phase is actually the beginning of something far more, an initiation into spiritual love.

Unlike the merging that often happens in emotional love, which can yield destructive results, the merging of spirits in spiritual love is felt as the quality of inspiration. Dante was inspired by the beauty of Beatrice. Their spirits came together without harm to either. Novalis was similarly inspired by Sophie, a young woman he met when she was but thirteen. She died several years later, but all of Novalis's work from then on was inspired by her. Her spirit was ever-present with him—in his poetry, his novels, and even in his practical work as a mining engineer. With Novalis, we clearly see that this marriage of spirits does not end with death. Novalis worked very hard to keep their spiritual connection present and conscious.

Such effort is a potent way of countering the presence of fear in the world. We can each do this in our own way. Do I care about the spiritual destiny of those I love? How can I be of spiritual help to them? Do I stand by, and for, the full reality of my beloved? What are the ways we can work together to witness the reality of love in the world? Living the answers to such questions works against the presence of fear in the world far more effectively than any external measures we might take.

Love of any sort brings difficulty. It hurts, burns, brings confusion, discomfort, keeps us awake at night, distracts us in the day, and even when it inspires us it does so with such intensity that we find ourselves chained to a force that will not let us loose. It seems to use everything within our soul for kindling, and it intensifies the small flame of the spirit to the point that the fire seems uncontrollable. Our small ego and personality can hardly stand the conflagration, and it seems we may go mad. Indeed, we can be destroyed if its strong presence goes unacknowledged. We may be unaware that we are undergoing the fires of purification that are utterly necessary to bring love into the world.

Many of today's counseling, therapy, and self-help practices pretend that there is something wrong with us if we cannot handle love. But who can? Therapy is no match for controlling the intensity of the flame, and instead it tries to counsel us on how to quench the fire. Such therapies advise us on getting along with our partner, finding out what men need and what women need, talking about it incessantly, strengthening egotism, concentrating on how to find satisfaction in sex, and how to avoid obsession. Trying to find success in love not only subdues love, it results in banal conventionality.

All attempts to make love conform to the rules, whether psychological, religious, or social, are oriented toward trying to harness love for our own purposes. Our ego tries to capture love. We want it for ourselves, to feel good, to experience the sentiment rather than the reality, and to feel self-satisfied rather than letting it work in its own mysterious ways to transform the world.

Human beings are the instruments of love, and love itself must form its instrument in it own fashion. It is thus necessary always to side with the love itself, regardless of what it may be putting the person through. The purpose of the purification process is to make possible the entry of love into the larger world. In the process of carrying forth love's purpose, we undergo significant transformations, accompanied by joy, sorrow, pain, and delight. We may mistake some aspects or other of the purification process for the goal of the process. We may think that the highest purpose of love in the world is for two people to love each other; that is one of the significant aspects of the purification process, but not its final end. If love flows between human beings, then it can also flow into the world. If the flow of love is restricted to what can occur between two human beings, even in its highest, most noble expression, we have unwittingly bound love.

Creative Love

If love flowed only among people, it would not necessarily result in stopping the advances of fear in all the regions we have considered. Love must flow also into the world, indeed become part of the very substance of the world. The mode of love that has the power to transform both human beings and the world is *creative love*. In order to get a glimpse of this sort of love we need to have sufficiently suffered the fires of love to come to the point of letting love form the instrument of our body. We have to be able to feel the surges of sexual love without either purging them or using them in a haphazard manner. This does not mean we must become celibate. The mark of having undergone the fires of sexual love is feeling joy in the body, joy in being sensate, joy in the presence of all things of the earthly world.

Second, we need to have sufficiently suffered the fires of love burning in the soul. Do we feel our separateness from those we love, feel that this separateness is guarded and protected by those who express love for us? In this separateness do we nonetheless feel united? Do we feel inner joy, amazement at the unending depth of the soul, feel called to guard and protect the depth of the soul of those we love? Do we know the soul realm, and no longer need to ask that someone give us a definition of what is meant by soul? Then, do the fires of love not only burn through the body and through the soul but also completely transform our thinking so that we experience the creative force of love, which inspires imaginative thinking and perceiving? When the various loves work through us and transform us, it becomes possible to get a glimpse of creative love.

Creative love works in strange and peculiar ways. Little can be said about its nature; we can know it only through its effects. Creative love works completely qualitatively; so does all love, but with the other modes there can be at least a referent that gives us a sense of something quite substantial—such as feeling love strongly or not so strongly, intensely or not so intensely. In creative love, the smallest act of love released into the world produces the same result as the largest act of love released into the world. Love does not exist as a quantity, so, strictly speaking, "large" and "small" do not apply. But large and small also describe qualities. If I am walking down the street and stop a moment to talk to a friend, and in the course of our little conversation, in a split second, the inner light of this person is revealed in her countenance, love flows through us and the spirit of the person is recognized. This small act of love is not just one of recognition; at that moment love is released into the world. Now imagine the daily work of someone like Mother Teresa. Her care for the suffering would definitely be considered a large act of love. Can we say, though, that the small act of love does less in the world than the large act of love? At first, the question seems ridiculous; it would seem without doubt that the large act of love does more.

Creative love entering the world cannot be measured in terms of results. Its intent is simply to flow into the world, and it is not subject to our judgment about what it may or may not do. In the two instances cited above, love flows into the world. Some are called to love in one way while others are called in a different way. While it is vital to your humanity to come to know how you are called to love and to be faithful to that way, one way cannot be considered more important than another. We might want to say that the love flowing through Mother Teresa affects many more people than the little encounter on the street corner. Such an evaluation only allows fear to step in; it makes us feel that only great souls such as Mother Teresa perform important acts of love. We simply cannot know the full effects of loving; not even Mother Teresa knew. There may be a more visible social result of what she did, but love does not rely on immediately visible social results. Creative love moves out into the world, beyond those through whom it may work. And as long as acts of love approach selflessness, love is released to act in the world.

Another truth about creative love: The stronger the intensity of love, the greater the increase of love in the world. As the instruments of love, it is possible for us to increase or decrease the intensity of love, but only indirectly, through focus of attention. We cannot focus love itself, we can only focus our attention. When our attention is at its fullest—that is, when our perception is oriented wholly toward what is before us, our body is at ease, and we are not occupied by any other thought or emotion—then love becomes more intense. When our attention is diffuse, love dissipates because of the inadequacy of the instrument. When we say a person loves intensely, we are speaking of the quality of his attention, not of his love.

Once we have a real feeling for the autonomy of love, once we realize that it does not originate from our own powers, our care can shift from the illusory question of whether I love rightly or strongly enough to caring for the instrument through which love comes into the world. The question is not what I can do to love better or more fully, but rather what I can do to be a proper vessel through which love can come into the world. The primary practice is to work constantly to be truly present. This act of attention requires that we move out of ourselves and enter fully into the heart and depth of what we attend to. We must be highly receptive to what we encounter, approach it without assumptions or judgments, letting the reality reveal itself to us. Then a second aspect of the act of attention comes into play. We struggle to find ways to express what we have experienced in the act of creative receptivity.

Another aspect of creative love is the capacity to surrender to love without losing oneself. If we surrender to the force of love blindly, we will lose ourselves in momentary ecstasy, an ecstasy so powerful that we become fixated on finding ways to reproduce this experience, not realizing that the ego is trying to capture love for its own pleasures. On the other hand, we do not have the ability to put our ego aside completely, not even after fuller capacities of imaginative cognition and soul life have been developed. What we can do is be aware of how our ego tries to capture the ecstasies of love, and gradually work at paying less and less attention to its demands. Ego constantly demands to be the center of our consciousness; it retains power by doing so. Ego also demands to be in control, and seeks to control even love. Ego further demands a feeling of self-satisfaction and self-importance. There is nothing wrong with possessing ego-consciousness; through it we become interested in the world. Initially, and for a long time thereafter, it acts only for our own gain, but our ego can become a true servant of love.

We come, then, to a final statement concerning creative love: the results of love in the world lie in the realm of the indeterminate, and the practice of love cannot be based in a desire for specific results. When love finds its way into the world, we cannot know how its transformative effects will work. We cannot direct its outcome because love is completely free. Even when love works through us toward another person, the effects of that love cannot be measured. In retrospect, for example, we might look back and see that the course of another person's life has changed, and that this has had something to do with our selfless love. So many other factors are involved, though, that we really cannot know for sure how the love has worked. Certainly, we cannot love expecting a specific result without the risk of our love turning into manipulation. The one thing we can be absolutely sure of is that love, released into the world to do its mysterious work, reduces the presence of fear everywhere.

Another world lies on the other side of fear. This new world is certainly no utopia, but it functions according to other laws and will offer us entirely different tasks with a very different kind of reward. In this world, we will find that love can operate at the center of all human concerns and, instead of atoms, can become the basic building block of the universe.

CHAPTER 8

Artistic Living

Strengthening our competence of soul, becoming aware of the tremendous power of fear in the world, living more from the region of the heart, guarding our consciousness from the efforts of doubling, developing imaginal cognition——all of these open the way to love. Still, one may ask, how can I tell when such efforts begin to bear fruit? They bear fruit from the moment we begin to shift our imagination even slightly. This shift begins when our encounters with fear go from being a burden to becoming a means through which we make the world holy. Fear desecrates, profanes, curses the world, and ultimately seeks to destroy it. Approached consciously, however, fear prompts us, through our inner capacities of imagination, to create something beautiful. This is why our stance toward fear must be one of neutralizing rather than destroying.

Although love can make a new world and effectively cancel the power of fear, it can do so only indirectly, through the beauty it inspires. Beauty, which will here be defined as the act of living artistically, is love made visible in the world. Artistic living consists of developing the ability to display, through our actions and attitudes, the power of soul and spirit in and for the world.

Through Love to Beauty

The shift of our imagination—from fighting against fear to bringing love into the world—comes not from the perception of less fear in the world, but rather from the perception of more beauty. Ugliness is the overcoat with which fear blankets the world, so if we are to counteract its presence, we have to connect with beauty. Working through fear to the central significance of love brings us to beauty as naturally as the darkness of night leads to the glow of dawn.

Beauty is an expansive concept, so we have to approach it by considering how it functions rather than trying to define its nature. It functions, first and foremost, as a question, a calling forth of the imagination to try to understand the depths of soul life. Once we have cleared away the torrent of fears that keep us so confined to the ugly, we will find a space within the heart that reverberates with the question: Why am I here? As long as we are running scared, the question cannot be heard, but if we listen carefully, we can feel the question being asked, as continuously as the beating of our hearts. This question is the inner standpoint from which the possibility of artistic living originates.

How should we answer this crucial question? Being alive means so much to each of us. Could we deny that? Well, some people would. The circumstances of their lives may lead them to say that they do not want to be here. This is fear speaking through them. As fears dominate the life of the soul, people no longer feel a lust for life. Clear away this fear, even a little, and the exuberance returns.

Should we answer by saying that we're here to seek happiness? A fool's errand, since our happiness will always be fleeting, especially if it depends on material wants and desires. Perhaps we believe we're here to prepare for the afterlife. We cannot forget, however, that we are now beings of Earth, and our lives here must also have a meaning. Perhaps we are here because Earth needs us. If we start with what meets our senses, if we are able to be present, we can experience Earth as a holy place. If we seek beauty in this direction and stand in awe of everything around us, love begins to find its larger purpose and fulfillment.

Our imagination is required to see that whatever we do should augment the beauty that surrounds us. All indigenous peoples live on Earth with this kind of respect for nature. In such cultures, Earth is not seen as a collection of animate beings and inanimate objects. Instead, all things are recognized as having their own soul and spirit, their own personality. Such an understanding is not regressive; it springs naturally from the act of releasing love into the world. But it's up to us to find our own way of engaging with beauty. As much as we may admire other cultures, we cannot replicate their efforts.

The path to beauty is found in the efforts we make to engage the holy as it exists all around us. From this point of view, beauty is an active presence, something we are called to, and not a passive object waiting for us to appreciate it. Because the word *beauty* is irreducible to a single meaning, we ought to start by clearing a little ground for how we will approach it. Although our principal concern will not be with art, or with aesthetics, or with the beauty of the natural world, nonetheless, we can learn something crucial about artistic living by describing a certain central aspect of all kinds of beauty.

Let us first consider the beauty of the natural world— the beauty of a sunset, a rainbow, a field of yellow flowers, a deer running through the woods, the majesty of a snow-capped mountain. When a thing appears beautiful it does so because it belongs together with the whole. The natural world functions as a whole, with each individual thing having its place within it. If you see a field of yellow flowers, it is in the context of a landscape; that landscape in turn exists in relation to other landscapes; and the blue sky overhead does not end at the boundaries of the field. If you walk into the field, cut a bouquet of flowers, and take them home, they still belong to the rain that fell on them, the ground that nurtured them, and the insects that thrived off their pollen. Beauty, rather than being something in itself, derives from these larger relationships. If we react in awe to a lion in a zoo, it is but a shadowy reflection of the beauty of a lion in his natural surroundings. We hardly recognize it, but it is so.

Both the vase of flowers and the lion in the zoo have been taken from their living context. Their beauty does not vanish entirely, because they are still here in the world and belong within the whole. But they can lose their beauty if not approached in a way that honors their context. We honor the flowers by arranging them, an act of artistic imagination which may add something to their beauty—or diminish it, if our arrangements are haphazard.

In the same way, human beings are part of a whole. We exist within a context that includes absolutely everything. Although we function as individuals, we are not isolated. We are inextricably bound up with others, with the world, and with the wider cosmos. Even our bodies exist only as a nexus of relationships; it is the place from which the world opens for us. We are in a relation with the air, with plant and animal life, with others, with the sun and the moon and the stars.

Our sense of individuality arises quite naturally with the emergence of ego consciousness. Only when fear enters to harden and crystallize our feelings of separation does this individuality come to feel like isolation. If we imagine that we are nothing more than a complex object inserted onto the stage of the world, we lose the very connections that sustain the life of the soul. Although it's possible to logically conceive of the human being in such isolation, it is not a fruitful way to live in the world.

We rely on a sense of the whole all the time. For example, the meaning of this sentence cannot be determined from the meaning of each word taken in isolation. Only as the words are read in relation to each other does the meaning of the sentence appear; the meaning of each word is thus dependent on the whole sentence. Likewise, when we awaken in the morning, we are part of a complete world, though we experience the meaning of that world only through the relationship of its many parts. As we discover the meaning of the totality, the whole in turn becomes an aspect of our perception of the parts. This imaginative consciousness of part-whole perception is key to the experience of beauty.

Art is different from the beauty of the natural world.

A work of art exists wholly in itself. Some may say that a work of art exists only within the context of all other works of art, in the way a flower in the field exists in relation to all the other things of the natural world. That is not correct. A painting, for example, is a complete, unique world unto itself. Every true painter knows this. A painter cannot paint the parts of a painting in isolation—he or she has to paint with the whole image in mind. A novice painter has difficulty doing this because it requires a different mode of consciousness. The painter uses one brushstroke at a time, but the final painting consists of more than the accumulation of those parts. A true painter knows when he has made a wrong stroke of the brush; he realizes when he has fallen into painting just a tree rather than a landscape. And whereas wholeness already exists within the natural world, in a work of art it must be made.

The notion that wholeness, or beauty, exists only in a transcendent realm belies the way that artists actually create. Art is not a matter of making the imaginative realm real. An artist takes what is real and gives it imaginative form. In art, the imaginative is not made real; the real is made imaginative.[1] An artistic image does not exist apart from the sensory presentation of itself.

Art does not exist for mere amusement, and when it tries to, it falls into decadence. Through art we experience spiritual pleasure, through the presence of something completely sensual. Such an artistic phenomenon satisfies because it is both a sensory object *and* an imaginal display of soul and spirit qualities. Beauty in a work of art is always something real and direct. Art does not merely point us toward beauty; because it is sensory, it is a direct link to the realm of the soul.

Most theories of artistic creation confuse the impulse of art with that of religion. They approach artistic creation as if it were founded in revelation, either from the heavens above or from the inner depths of the soul. If this were so, a work of art could never be satisfying because a huge gap exists between the revelation and its expression. Just as when we have an insight and try to convey it in words, and feel the inadequacy of our words, the notion of bringing down inspiration from the spiritual world will always result in feelings of artistic inadequacy.

We could think of religion and art as two currents working in opposite directions. Religion is based on spiritual revelations that become coded in texts and rituals. Art, at least in our time, is based on human efforts to elevate our sensory experience to the spirit realms. Rudolf Steiner speaks of art as a "reversed cult." He means, in effect, that the artist's task is to create something of a spiritual nature from sensory materials, while the task of religion is to bring the soul and spirit domains into sensory expression.

Our task of making ourselves whole resembles the

artistic model of creation more than with the religious model. Most people who become interested in soul work do so out of a religious need, having given up on organized religion as a means of caring for the individual soul. Jung's work, for example, stemmed from his difficulties with religion, which led him to establish a spiritual basis for the psyche. Instead of listening to sermons, Jung said, one ought to listen to one's dreams and work at knowing the inner gods as they are revealed through archetypal patterns.

I daresay, knowing it will be controversial, that the psychology of Jung has not had, and most likely will not have, much effect on the process of bringing beauty into the world. Although his psychology has the potential to renew religious sensibility, it has had virtually no effect on the making of beauty in the world. There is no Jungian architecture, drama, poetry, music, or other forms of beauty stemming from his work. He came closest to understanding soul work that is world-oriented with his study of alchemy, but even there he missed the mark because he failed to see that alchemy was an art, concerned with real, sensory materials and their transformation into spiritual qualities through human agency. He placed no value on what the alchemists actually did and looked only at their psychic makeup.

I am not attempting to dismiss Jung and the larger field of depth psychology. His capacities of observation were highly developed, and we have to be thankful for his scientific training and dogged determination to know through observation, more than through his mystical inclinations. This aspect of Jung serves as a model for any true soul work. Approaching the question of how we can go about making ourselves whole depends completely on a capacity for careful observation.

Toward Living Artistically

The force of love in the world can tip the scales against fear, but only when it is released into the world, and its release relies on elevating the sensory and life processes into acts of the soul. The twelve senses and the seven life processes are the materials to be shaped in such a way that the whole of our love shines through them.

What each of the arts does, in its own particular way, is to elevate the senses to the soul and spirit domain. Although the different arts don't correspond to just one or another of the senses and life processes, each does center on uplifting a specific sense. Then the rest of the senses, drawing the life process along, gather in support of that sense.[2] Our task will be to look at the arts, see how they shape the senses, and then inquire how we might in our own life engage in similar creative acts by making ourselves part of a whole.

Dance and Balance

Dance works most centrally with our sense of balance. At the very least, this sense gives us the ability to walk upright, but beyond that it has undreamed of possibilities. Imagine being present at a beautiful dance performance. The dancers move freely, more freely than we ever could. The dancers do not just use their sense of balance; they have worked long and hard to shape their sense of balance, to elevate it to an art by endowing it with form—the form of the dance. If the dancers fail to give themselves over to the shape of the dance, we may have something that looks like dance—it may even be technically excellent—but artistically, such dance appears stilted and forced.

Dancers must not let their own individual desire enter the dance. This does not mean suppressing desire, but holding it in check so that it does not infect the dance. When we dance—ordinary dance, not dance as an art—we play with our sense of balance and express our own desire for pleasure. If an artistic dancer were to express his or her desires in such a personal way, the whole dance would be ruined. The dancer's individual desires express the ego concerns of the dancer rather than the dance itself. The true dancer does not love dancing as much as the dance.

In our daily life, we are not usually aware of our sense

of balance until we slip on the ice and lose it, or go on a wild carnival ride and find our stomachs in our throats. More to the point, however, when fear is strong, it places our stomachs in our throats, disturbing our sense of balance whether or not we're on a carnival ride. Even when fear is not immediately present, it can continue to reverberate in the soul, disturb our thinking, or introduce the double, and in each case our sense of balance is disturbed. We may not notice it because the body has adjusted. Nonetheless, we live "out of balance." But, if we have worked somewhat on the difficulties of fear so that it no longer separates us from the immediate qualities of the world, our sense of balance will begin to be much more refined.

It would be quite helpful, when we wake up in the morning, to begin the day by paying a moment's worth of attention to balance. During sleep, our soul and spirit have somewhat left our body, and through the night they traverse spaceless and timeless regions. In the morning it takes a while for us to adjust again to the surrounding world. Usually, finding balance goes unnoticed, just as much as our being off balance goes unnoticed. Sometimes, a particularly powerful dream makes it difficult to feel balanced for the rest of the day. Such instances show, in an exaggerated way, how we must bring ourselves into a state of balance each day. When we feel "spaced out," it can be helpful to imagine the force of

gravity pulling us to Earth. When we feel heavy and slug-
gish, it can be helpful to meditate on something of a buoy-
ant, spiritual nature.

While finding our sense of balance won't always call us
to become dancers, we may indeed feel ourselves wanting
to dance. Rather than just noticing this feeling and letting
it go, we can use it as an opportunity to become more
acutely aware of our bodily posture. Doing this, we may
find ourselves amazed at our ability to stand upright, and
notice how honoring this posture puts us into alignment
with the sky above and Earth below. In this alignment, we
may experience being more in tune with our aspirations,
which seem more related to the sky, and our desires, which
seem more related to Earth. We may also become much
more aware of the subtle things that throw us off balance,
things that have to do with fear, and will begin to know in
a sensory way when they are knocking at our door, even
when they approach in ways that, on the surface, look nothing like fear at all. These qualities of balance will not be felt
without some prior effort to offset fear, nor will they be
felt if we have not matured in the dimension of love.

Mime and Movement

Movement is the sense through which we experience the
motions of the body. The organs for this sense are the mus-
cles. When I move my arm, this movement within is regis-
tered by the nerves in the muscle tissue, and I feel it. I

experience not only the larger movements of arms and legs but smaller movements of the body as well—the turning of my neck, the in-and-out rhythm of my chest as I breathe, the shifting of my eyes, even the blinking of my eyelids. The sense of movement gives us an inner, bodily feeling of freedom, but more is involved with this feeling than simply being able to move from place to place. The smaller movements in particular, such as those of the eyes, make it possible for us to feel a sense of freedom and mobility, even if we don't move our bodies in any significant way.

We can learn much from our sense of movement when it is elevated to a form of art with mime. Mime uplifts the sense of movement into an imaginative form. Though mime has become a rare (and not always highly regarded) art form, and has lingered on mostly as a kind of amusement, it is actually a high art. The difference between dance and mime is interesting to note: mime is more two-dimensional than dance. Even though it is performed in three dimensions, it is as if the action occurs on a flat surface, something akin to the mime working against a pane of glass. The quality of movement itself is thus enhanced, given form, clothed in imagination. The objects and people with whom the mime interacts are invisible, and thus we are allowed to focus our attention more vividly on the act of movement itself.

In ordinary life, our sense of movement is greatly affected by the presence of fear. We become frozen, immobile, feel constrained, trapped. The thrashings of fear can actually take us over and pull us into their chaotic motions. Someone caught in the throes of fear might begin running wildly, arms flailing, screaming. While we are most aware of this bodily disruption when fear is strong, it nonetheless affects this sense all the time, to the point that we may no longer experience the feeling of being free. When this happens, we have to extricate ourselves from this influence by developing the soul, strengthening the imagination, and cultivating the four kinds of love. The idea is to let love move us, rather than thoughtlessly engaging in activities that seem purposeful but actually reveal our abdication to fear.

For the mime, even the slightest gesture is filled with significance, with the beauty of the movement itself. When a deep awareness of movement occurs in daily life, we have a sense of grace about us, a sense of elegance. Conscious movement, as shown in practices such as tai chi, attunes us to the life energies of the world, teaching us how to circumvent fear, to bend with it like a supple willow rather than trying to resist it head-on, certain to be broken.

Graceful movement, taken up artistically, implies that motion is coordinated with whatever presents itself in the world. If we surround ourselves, however, with only mechanical contrivances, a certain kind of coordination also occurs, though here the objects strongly shape our movement, and spontaneity can be lost. This can happen not just with mechanical devices, but with any harsh arrangement of our surroundings.

I remember once deciding to take a walk in Anaheim, California, while attending a convention there. As I went around the corner, I was shocked to see that the sidewalk seemed to run straight for miles and miles, unbroken. Undaunted, I set out, and after several miles found myself curiously unable to simply stop, turn around, and go back. My movement had become shaped by the long, narrow strip of concrete. It was as if I had become hypnotized by the repetitious sameness of the concrete as well as the pace of walking it. I lost a sense of freedom in that setting. In such surroundings one can hardly practice making movement into an art form.

When we are out in the natural world, walking through a terrain that shifts up and down—a stroll in a hilly woodland, say—walking becomes more artful quite naturally. Few of us, however, have the opportunity to take such daily walks. Developing an imagination of movement becomes necessary. We can begin doing so by noticing how the feeling of freedom disappears when the surroundings are mechanical. We can notice, too, how in such situations we become much more subject to fear. On my walk in Anaheim, despite the fact that it was broad daylight, I began to feel fear. As cars sped past me, I feared one of them would veer off the road and strike me; I feared that a car full of rowdy gang members might see me and in some way threaten me. Even in that situation, in which my movement was so influenced by the concrete, I found that when I became aware of the act of walking, my fears subsided.

With artistic living, we take up the responsibility for what we look at in the world. If I see only moving cars, crowds of people hustling on the sidewalk, mechanical shapes and forms, hard edges of buildings, all of these dull the experience of freedom. I can balance this by watching the movement of clouds in the sky, the swaying of trees in a light breeze, or by focusing on the way a particular person moves, how she gestures with her hands, tilts her head, how she looks at me, whether with her eyes focused on me or wandering all around the room. These small things make a tremendous difference: I have become the shaper, rather than the one being shaped. I remain awake and alert in my sense of movement. Gradually, I will begin to see patterns and arrangements, unified motion consisting of many parts, but also something whole. Even my thinking is different—not so fragmented, more fluid—and I am more aware of the thinking of others.

Painting and Vision
A painter takes color and form and arranges them so that we see an image that reveals the inner depth of the world.

The painter's visual imagination may turn outward, seeing beyond the surface of things into their inner qualities. It may also turn inward, seeing within the soul itself. In either case, the painter is able to see that color and form are living beings.

Where we may see just a red object, a static form with a colored surface, the painter feels the activity of such an object and seeks to capture it on the canvas. We may look at a field of sunflowers and admire its beauty, but van Gogh saw such an intensity of life in the vibrant yellow against the blue of the sky, swirling into each other, creating each other, that to make an image of what he saw all but killed him. With such vision, the painter not only sees what is before her and seeks to represent it, but also views a unified whole of color and form and is conscious of the fact that it is the soul making this perception. This vision arises not from the detached point of view of an omniscient spectator, but from a merging of the soul's imaginal consciousness with the outer world. Regardless of the content of what the painter paints, this sort of seeing is involved.

That kind of observation captures reality more thoroughly than science, because it takes into account the viewer, not just as a theoretical construct but as an actuality. Viewed in this way, the world no longer consists of things and events, but of living beings that display their inner nature only by being seen through the soul.

Because we do not ordinarily see the world the way a painter does, the things of the world are diminished. Their inner qualities are sacrificed, and they are used up rather than praised. What would you be if no one ever really saw you? At first, you would feel lonely and isolated, as if you did not belong in the world. You might respond by trying to exaggerate your presence but eventually would simply wither away. You might not literally die, but you would become more like an automaton than a being endowed with a soul.

If we do not look deeply into the world and see its life in ways that are analogous to a painter's vision, the world too withers away and dies, even though, on the surface, it seems to go on as usual. The oceans become infested with oil because we really cannot see that they not only contain life but also are alive. The forests are ruthlessly cut away because we can no longer really see a tree. Vast areas of land give way to huge shopping centers because we cannot see the living landscape.

For anyone who begins to really see the world, vision can be painful. Although it may not be immediately apparent, most of the world around us is now dead. To bring our capacity to see to life, even a little, by taking the time and the care to look, shows us with tragic clarity how much fear already dominates the world. It takes spiritual courage to really look, but our efforts to see through the eyes of the soul without recoiling in horror will not go unnoticed by the world.

Poetry and Speech

Poetry concerns the speech sense, and it allows a unique form of human expression. With poetry, language is uplifted to the spirit realm, where it exists not as mere words or concepts, but as pure action. The language becomes alive and real. It *does* rather than means. Poetry does not just describe an inner, personal feeling that one may have, nor does it describe how we feel in relation to the world. A poem is pure speech and requires that we perceive it not simply through the intellect but through the sense of speech. And who is speaking? Not really the poet, for the poet is no more than the vehicle for the poem, which exists on its own. The world speaks in poetry, whether it's the inner world or the outer world. The words of the poet transform the silent voice of the world so that it takes on human language and becomes an expressive gesture.

In our lives, we often hear only the content of what someone says. We can, though, focus more consciously on the rhythm, the pauses, the silences, and can hear what is not said in what is being said. To listen in this way we have to hear through our whole body, not just through our ears; and we have to listen to what the body is receiving, not just to what the mind recognizes. We can also speak not just what we think and feel but jump into the abyss of not-knowing, and there let language come to us and speak through us. We can be far more conscious of metaphor, likeness, analogy, and even use ordinary language to break through common speech patterns by always trying to say what we do not know rather than what we already know.

Silence is the womb of speech, and speaking artistically means speaking only when there is a real need to say something beyond our ordinary opinions and judgments. When a thought comes to you, keep it back, do not utter it at once, but nourish it in the darkness of holy silence. Then this thought can attract the speech of the world, like a magnet. What needs saying needs space to fructify. The intent here is not to always try to speak of important things, but to form ourselves into a unity with the world in our speaking, so that speaking expresses not only our will but the will of the world, the will of the cosmos, the will of the soul. Our own little egotism chatters away incessantly, an indication that we are filled with anxiety, trepidation, and fear, and our speech does no more than release it onto others. Artistic speech can change the world by letting the world, speaking through us, change us.

Music and Hearing

Music centers in the sense of hearing. It is not, however, an imitation of sounds heard in the world. The songs of birds, for example, are melodious sounds, but they are not true music. Hearing must be elevated to the realm of the soul to become music, giving sound a new, imaginative form. This musical imagination requires more than momentary flights of inspiration. The musician must live, with the depth of his soul, in the house of inspiration. Music is quite literally the sound of inspiration resounding within the soul. The only other domain where inspiration can be so directly entered is mathematics.

The music we hear is not quite the same as what the musician or the composer hears within the soul. And yet when the soul's inspiration is made into music, we enter the state of the qualities of the music itself; songs can fill us with love, tragedy, or joy. When music fills us completely, no room is left to think about what the sounds mean. Live music does this much more effectively than recorded music, not only because we sit and give full attention to an orchestra or a singer but also because recordings do strange things to the music. Recordings flatten physical space, making it difficult to hear how the flutes come from the center at the back, the violas from the right in the front. We can no longer sense that music flows through people and instruments, that they are as much a part of the music as the sound themselves.

The realm of music teaches us a great deal about inspired living. We feel inspired when we are what we do, when there is no room left over in our being for random thoughts or fantasies. Then we are in tune with our actions, in harmony with our purposes, and do things in the right rhythm, with the right timing. It is necessary to listen closely to hear what inspires us. Once we have an understanding of its source, then whatever is at hand can become an instrument through which this inspiration enters the world. I may be writing, or teaching, or selling shoes, or cutting the grass; any of these activities can feel inspired. Whatever we do is then done beautifully, like an art. Inspiration is not just for the poets and painters and novelists. Although they live in such states more intensely and perhaps more continuously, with practice, so can we. What the artists show us is that coming to live in more inspired ways takes discipline and effort. The old saw that genius is ten percent inspiration and ninety percent perspiration is an unavoidable truth. We all have that ten percent, but few develop what is needed to bring it into action.

Just as musicians have to tune their instruments, warm up, learn basic exercises, and practice over and over, every day without fail, we have to work in life to make ourselves available for inspiration. It is not just a matter of receiving; everything has to be just right for it to happen. Our instrument is the whole of our being—body, soul, and spirit. If my body is doing one thing while my soul is off into some fantasy or another, and my spirit does not even seem to be here, then a major tuning is in order. Stress and fear have to be cleared so that one can feel completely at home in one's body.

What does this warming up consist of? Right breathing, relaxation, exercise, right eating, focus of attention. For the soul, some basic exercises, such as the image-making exercise described in the first chapter. And for the spirit, a meditation. For example, take a simple phrase— such as "We always live in the light"—and meditate on it. This does not mean thinking about it, but taking it into the higher regions of consciousness and letting it dwell there. Focus on emphasizing one of the words (*"We* always live in the light"), then another ("We always live in the *light*"). The intention of this exercise is to gradually allow the whole of the sentence to be centered on a single word. Then, the sentence will gradually come to exist as a whole rather than as a string of words. Such daily practices tune the instrument of our being and reveal to us that spirit does not exist in the same temporal sequence that we live in. No matter how advanced we become, just like the musician, we must continue to do these basic exercises.

Having practiced so long and so hard, the moment

comes when the musician steps onto the stage and must play. We, in an analogous manner, enter into the activities of the day, which can now be re-visited as a serious kind of playing. Take each day as a performance, a performance of the unity of our being as body, soul, and spirit in harmony with the world. When the performance has been completed, we may leave the stage and practice some more. Life becomes a matter of listening.

Literature and the Unity of Sensing

The art of literature may seem to belong with poetry, or at least to be a part of the poetic imagination, but there's a distinction. Poetry is meant to be spoken, whereas literature is read, which makes it an interior art. The literary imagination works inside us to elevate all of our senses to the level of the soul. If a flower is described in a work of literature, the smell and touch of the flower appear to the imagination while reading. Of course, we do not literally smell roses when we read of two lovers kissing at night in the midst of a rose garden. Our imagination can, however, recall the sensation of smelling a rose, and fill our being with that sensation as we read.

In literature, we enter a world in which all the senses, together, are elevated to the level of imagination. In addition, the imaginary sensory world of literature does interesting things with time. A story has a sequence—a beginning, a middle, and an end. This sequence does not always proceed in a straightforward manner. Sometimes the story begins at the end, there may be flashbacks, time gets mixed up. Time becomes an imaginary reality, which is nonetheless felt as real. A historical novel might traverse centuries, and readers may feel they have lived through those centuries.

Finally, a work of literature has a plot. Through the presentation of events in the imaginary world of time and space we are introduced to the soul destinies of the characters involved. We see the motives and intentions of the characters, how they are moved by mysterious forces of fate, sense where freedom is possible and where it is not. We see the soul in action rather than merely contemplating the definition of the soul. All literature falls into four great movements of the soul—epic, tragic, comic, and lyric.[3] All sorts of mixtures of these soul patterns occur, but they are always variations of these four worlds of the soul. In the epic, we are shown the heroic movement of the soul; in tragedy, the fallen character of human beings; in comedy, the world is redeemed; and in the lyric, we get a taste of the imagination of paradise.

The reading of literature involves far more than entertainment. Perhaps more than any other art form, it teaches us how to live. With great literature, we are not instructed didactically but learn by being taken into an imagination of life itself, developing our soul into an adequate organ for facing the world. We are changed by being introduced to birth, death, love, fate, family, hope, despair, conflict, conscience, success, failure. While we experience all of these qualities in life, we do not always have the capacity to see when and how they arise, and the ultimate significance of actions. In literature, we see what the thirst for power leads to, how love changes lives forever, the consequences of unresolved conflict.

The lessons learned from literature cannot be taken into life and applied directly as sources for values, ethics, morals. Rather, literature informs our sensibilities—it makes our sensing whole—and thereby strengthens the soul to meet the forces of fear with the absolute certainty that the human enterprise, and all it is meant to become, can prevail.

Sensing and the Life Processes
Although our senses ordinarily function quite independently of one another, they are nevertheless able to operate in unison without becoming confused. Seeing does not interfere with hearing; hearing is quite separate from taste; touch is separate from balance; and so on. Each of the senses, though, is imbued with life. The eye, for example, is more than just an optical apparatus for bringing pictures of the outer world to us. Life flows into the act of vision. Life consists of very specific processes— breathing, warming, nourishing, secreting, maintaining,

growing, and reproducing—but these life processes are not as neatly separated as the senses. They flow into each other.

The more habitual sensing becomes, the more the life processes recede from our senses, turning sensing into mere nerve processes—instinctual, automatic, and without conscious feeling. Taking up the practice of artistic living allows life to flow back into the senses.[4] When we look at our everyday surroundings, for example, we see all sorts of colors all the time. Although they vary in intensity, they are perceived simply as colors. Colors in a painting have a heightened quality of liveliness. The sense organ of vision is infused with more life than is ordinarily the case, and it brings all of our senses into active relation with each other. In our perception of color and form, we also, in a subtle way, touch the color, and even taste and smell it, though touching, tasting, and smelling in this sense are imagistic soul qualities rather than mere physical processes.

As more life enters the senses, the life processes also undergo a change. The processes of breathing, warming, and nourishing all have to do with the body's relation to the outer world. In breathing, there is an ongoing exchange between the inner body and the outer world. With warming, the inner heat generated within the body relates to the temperature in the world. With nourishing, we ingest nutrients, and they are converted into the substance of the body. As these three life processes enter more strongly into sensing, a different way of knowing the world begins to surface. An artist, for example, does not know the world the way other people know the world. The artist perceives images, lives in images, knows through images. In imaginal knowing, the relation between the body and the world is vividly felt. Warmth becomes more than temperature; it becomes the soul quality of intense, warm interest in the world. And sensing itself becomes experienced as nourishment for the soul. If we live artistically, we know through our body, which certainly includes thinking, but is now full-bodied thinking.

The life processes of secretion, maintenance, growth, and reproduction have more to do with the body's inner life than with its ongoing relation to the outer world. Secretion eliminates what remains after the nourishment has been absorbed by the body. Maintenance is the action of the absorbed nutrients that sustain bodily life. Growth concerns the ongoing changes in the cells and organs of the body, through which the body is continually dying and regenerating. Reproduction concerns the processes of the body involved with creating new life. Together, these life processes imbue the body with a felt sense of depth, a feeling of our body as dynamic, changing, fertile, even seething with desire. In artistic perception, these processes also flow more strongly into the senses, and the result is sensing intensified with feeling. The everyday obviousness of things around us takes on a quality of transparency. Something shines through them. We experience beauty shining through the mundane. The things around us and our most intimate self are grasped together. The subject—object dichotomy is transcended.

Artistic living does not mean simply having stronger feelings; it means noticing how the colors and shapes of everything form a world of feeling. We can be deeply moved by the deep red of a rose, the shape of architecture, the dark shadows cast by a flickering candle, the form of a simple, well-made bowl, because they themselves embody feeling.

The whole realm of the arts can be our most valuable educator toward artistic living that can free the soul from fear. In this realm the sensibility of the body unites with the imaginative force of the soul and the creative power of the spirit. Because we live in a highly materialistic culture, we think that the domains of soul and spirit are completely separate from the physical sphere. Only because materialism rules do we imagine soul as an inner, subjective state removed from the world, and spirit-experience as a completely disembodied condition. Fear relies on keeping these parts of the whole separated. It does not demand that soul and spirit be excluded, only kept apart, isolated. It then allows for certain kinds of peculiar soul and spirit experiences. Spirit is allowed as forms of "mystical materialism," often taking the form of spiritual "energies," or "messages" from beyond, or visitation by angels. Soul is allowed in dream life, or perhaps the therapy room, or in myths and symbology, but not in daily life. As long as the senses are deadened, the wholeness of our being remains compartmentalized, and fear is left free to roam at will.

When body, soul, and spirit are allowed their unity once again through freeing the soul from fear, these three aspects of our being support the expression of truth, beauty, and goodness in the world.[5] These are the three great ideals of humanity. They always have been, but we no longer have a concrete feeling for these three ideals— at most they carry an abstract value, to be argued over by the philosophers and the academics. Only by living artistically will these three ideals become realities and overcome fear in the world. If one of them is degraded, so will the others be; each relies on the health and vitality of the other.

We feel the truth by being in a closer, more imaginative relationship to reality through the wholeness of the body. Truth, in turn, strengthens our feeling of bodily existence. We feel an inner strength, something quite physical, when we feel we have stood for what is true. We cannot always know the truth, and in fact, in this complex world, we almost never do. We do better, though, by working toward a feeling for the truth, experienced in a bodily way, than by making pronouncements and taking our opinions as fact.

We find beauty by having the discipline and sensibility to perceive the whole instead of the parts. The presence of beauty is what allows us to feel the life of the body — to feel fingertips, brow, inner warmth, sensations, and emotions — and experience these qualities in an ongoing way, not just now and then when they bubble up to the surface. Artistic living returns us to beauty. Beauty, in turn, gives back the presence of joy to the body.

We discover goodness by acting on our heightened soul awareness, which has come from our awakening to truth and beauty. Goodness brings the will into action. We do the good, not just feel it. Goodness consists of the capacity to go beyond ourselves, beyond our self-interests, and enter into the lives of others, doing so not intrusively but selflessly. Artistic living educates us into the subtlety necessary to be concerned for others without imposing our own view of what we think may be good for them, but instead letting what is needed reveal itself.

CHAPTER 9

Fear and Consciousness

Using the wings of imagination to find our way to love, and then bringing that love into the world through beauty, might seem to describe fully how we can counter the pervading influence of fear. However, to stop there risks leaving the reader with an aesthetic rather than an imaginative understanding of the need for a continued struggle with the ever-growing specter of fear. No place where fear might find a foothold should be left unexamined, and the still unopened room where fear plays havoc is our own consciousness. This room may be the most difficult to enter, not because the fear we will find there is especially pernicious, but because we must use consciousness itself to address it. Since we not only experience personal instances of fear but also live in a world pervaded by it, we are all subjected to detrimental influences from an early age. Fear thus becomes insinuated into the very structure of thought, memory, and perception, forming a background of our consciousness.

What does conscious life consist of? This is not an easy question, but to get us started I want to distinguish consciousness from awareness. In our waking life, we sense both our body and the surrounding world; we are also aware of our inner states, our feelings and emotions. And yet our awareness of these things does not mean we are conscious of them. A cognitive element, what Georg Kuhlewind calls pure thinking, is essential to becoming fully aware of our awareness.[1] Conscious life functions normally when we reflect on ourselves and the surrounding world at the same time, without the balance tipping too far in either direction. If we become too self-aware, consciousness slips into egotism, whereas if we are completely outward looking, we become blind to our own participation in conscious life.

Another central aspect of consciousness is memory. Memory contributes significantly to our sense of personal identity and, along with the cognitive element of consciousness, is what differentiates perception from mere sensing. When a young child first sees a brown furry thing moving across the floor, for example, he or she senses something barely distinguishable from the swarm of light, color, and sound surrounding it. Over time, the child will find meaning in the sensory experience and learn to identify the thing as a dog; once this identity is established, the experiences the child has with the dog will become an aspect of memory. This allows the child to perceive other dogs without having to learn their meaning anew.

Another aspect of consciousness is the intellect, which involves the ability to utilize aspects of ordinary consciousness—cognition, memory, and perception—to make inferences concerning ourselves and the world around us. Other activities can enter into this awareness, such as feelings, imagination, inspiration, and intuition, but these activities originate in the deeper recesses of soul life and the higher processes of spirit life, and are precisely what fear seeks to banish from ordinary waking consciousness. Our day-to-day existence consists primarily of ego consciousness, a term that describes the highly restricted range of consciousness that we have come to understand as normal. Without the full range of conscious activities, however, being "normal" in this way is decidedly abnormal.[2]

Ego consciousness involves the strong tendency to relate all of our conscious activities toward self-feeling, self-preservation, and self-pleasure, manipulating others and the surrounding world for its own gratification.

When the need for power is too strong, ego consciousness turns into egotism, and this little domain of soul life becomes extremely self-protective. When feeling, fantasy, imagination, inspiration, or intuition momentarily rises into consciousness, the ego may feel threatened. We generally experience these domains of consciousness as coming to us unbidden, under their own volition—they may defy logic, coherence, and understanding, and no longer seem subject to the ego's power and control. Once they've entered, they can become more powerful than our "normal" conscious states, threatening to usurp our little island of ego, and if they persist in intruding, it may feel as if we are going crazy. In actuality, the possibility of becoming fully human is announcing itself.

Ordinary consciousness allows us to know ourselves only as deeply as our personal memories, to perceive only through the senses, and to think only with the intellect. Our everyday awareness does not allow us to be imaginally conscious, to participate directly in inspiration or intuition. We may access these realms of consciousness momentarily through meditation, dreamwork, guided-imagination work, or other kinds of "consciousness-raising" practices, but they are not part of our daily fare. The ego sustains the illusion that it alone constitutes practical consciousness, denying that it lives perpetually in fear, and we are shut off from the modes of consciousness that could show us the way through a fearful world.

When strong feelings, fantasies, or inspirations do come to us, they are typically associated with fear because we no longer feel centered in the ego. Suppose, for example, I have a dream in which I am being chased by five large men wielding knives, shouting that they are going to kill me when they catch me. I awaken in great fear. The situation here is decidedly different from having five men with knives chase me down the street in waking life. With the latter, my life is threatened. In the dream, ego consciousness is threatened and feels powerless. I am presented with something entirely unfamiliar, something ordinary consciousness is unable to deal with. Jungian psychology would say that the dream signals the necessity of developing an experiential appreciation of the shadow, another way of saying that fear would be alleviated by developing imaginative consciousness.

The connection between fear and ego consciousness cannot be understood simply in terms of the ego's separation from the wider, deeper, and higher aspects of consciousness. Such a view leads naturally to the notion that to be free of fear, ego consciousness must be eradicated. Many spiritual traditions put forth exactly this view. However, ego consciousness cannot be equated with fearful consciousness. The central aspect of this mode of awareness is not fear, but freedom, since it represents our ability to make conscious choices, to experience a sense of identity, and to have individual power.

Fear installs itself within us in order to make us forgetful of this most central and creative aspect of ego consciousness. It hides itself very well, taking us over so completely that the ego is threatened by the possibility of the intrusion of other kinds of consciousness. When thus threatened, the ego makes it appear as if threat is coming from without, when actually our fear is hidden within ego consciousness. A quite elaborate system of denial characterizes the tactics of fear installed within ego consciousness, which betrays an intelligence that seems to go beyond our own cleverness. It's a testament to fear's shrewdness and autonomy that we are not even aware of this denial.

The narrow, restricted range of ordinary ego consciousness that characterizes it in the presence of fear has one primary formal characteristic—it takes everything it comprehends literally. For example, from the viewpoint of ego consciousness, money means only dollars and cents. For imaginative consciousness, however, money means not just dollars and cents, but power, value, connection with the world, a gift from the gods, filthy lucre, and many other images, all present simultaneously. Ego consciousness has little capacity for metaphor, analogy, likeness, inner contradiction, image, or story. These elements, which have to do with imaginative forms, are allowed to intrude into consciousness only in the form of entertainment, amusement, or, from time to time, a kind of play.

The quality of literal-mindedness, of taking things in only one way rather than two or more ways simultaneously, has a deadening effect on what ego consciousness comprehends. What is alive, in motion, dynamic, moving, changing, fleeting, ephemeral, evanescent—characteristics of all reality, visible and invisible—is frozen into stillness, as if a snapshot could signify a whole world. Our ego perception cannot match the fullness of reality. It is the fear that has such a deadly effect on what our consciousness comprehends.

One-Dimensional Fear

If fear is the covert commander of ordinary consciousness, its principal tactic is to flatten reality and make all experience appear to lie in a single plane, the plane of literalism. Whatever cannot be flattened is shunned from "normal" reality—the mind labels it "weird," say, or classifies it as a psychological illness. A secondary tactic of fear in this domain consists of taking all that arises from the soul and immediately appropriating it to the status of the ego. In dream interpretation, for example, the ego either disregards the dream as frivolous or tries to reach a conclusion about its meaning, looking for clues beyond what the dream itself presents. The "real" meaning of the dream is thought to be available through psychological interpretation, which takes the wide range of soul life and narrows it to the level of ego. The living quality of the dream is effectively killed through such interpretation. Likewise, feelings are understood as possessions—as "my" feelings—rather than as something coming to us from a realm entirely different from ordinary consciousness. If, for example, we say "I feel great sadness," this signals the ego's appropriation of the domain of feeling. It is more accurate to say "a great sadness has visited me." If an inspiration comes, we believe that we have engendered the original idea on our own. As a result of such appropriation, nothing new or unfamiliar can enter the mind, because fear-directed ego consciousness can only let in what it already comprehends.

One might think that depth and breadth of soul life go on anyway, that fear cannot destroy the soul, and that inspiration is always available to those willing to remain open. First, however, it is important to realize that soul is not an entity, not even of the most subtle kind. Soul is a capacity that functions by weaving disparate and polar qualities together into a single form, the form of images.

Such images are not pictures to be looked at, not even in an inner way, but are the act of picturing itself. Further, the soul's action of picturing does not represent a reality that exists elsewhere—it is not a picturing of something not present—but rather a presentation of realities that remain invisible to ordinary consciousness. When fear gets inside these soul capacities, it can destroy them.

Look at a rose, for example. You sense a red form with a certain quality of smell, but since you have sensed such a thing many times before and were at some point told that this form is a flower with the name "rose," your memory gives the sensation meaning. Perhaps you are a gardener and have accumulated an intellectual knowledge about such flowers. You also enjoy the beauty and the smell of the rose. These experiences all belong to the realm of ordinary consciousness. If you now turn away from what you perceive, you can picture the rose, but this activity is captured by, and limited to, ordinary ego consciousness, which results in our merely looking at an inner picture. The living soul quality of the rose has already disappeared; it is lost to ordinary consciousness, for even here fear has entered and successfully killed the life of the rose. The fear existing within ego consciousness blocks the full depth of the imagining of the rose. Only a shadow of its true reality remains, and yet we are completely oblivious to what has happened.

A rose far surpasses being only a physical reality; it is that, of course, but it is also so much more. If, instead of turning away from the flower and trying to capture an inner picture, you concentrate the mind on re-creating every aspect of the rose's reality, you will begin to experience far more subtle qualities. These qualities can hardly be put into words—the extraordinary delicacy of the petals, the deep red hue, which does not at all appear as a colored object but as the very life of the color red. You become aware of the particular form of the petals, which are not so much a shape but a gesture. And the smell goes right to the very center of your heart, a smell so deep you can taste it, a joining of fragrance with color.

Through this act of concentration, we approach the reality of the rose, and it is just the beginning of a true soul experience. The full imagination of the rose can be gone into further; one could take a lifetime to do so and never exhaust the reality of the rose. One can go well beyond the flower and imagine the leaves, the stem, the thorns, the roots, the surrounding earth, the connection between the rose and the sky, the sun, the moon, the stars.

Further, the qualities of the rose that are usually taken as symbolic—purity, love, tenderness—can be made real by carefully concentrating on our inner image-making. Gertrude Stein said, "Rose is a rose is a rose," which is understood by ego consciousness to mean that one should not take a rose as having many meanings—a rose is just a rose. Imaginal consciousness understands this as saying that the reality of the rose goes on and on and on.

If you attempt this concentration exercise, the first thing you experience may be fear. When we try to set aside ordinary ego consciousness, the fear within that consciousness comes forward to form a boundary, as if warning us not to cross over into a wider, more expansive consciousness. The fear acts very quickly, though, and you may not feel it directly. Instead, you may feel that you cannot keep your concentration on an inner image without other thoughts, feelings, and images surging in. Or you may judge the exercise to be ridiculous, or feel frustrated at the attempt, or become overwhelmed. Fear hovers near all such reactions. If one has experienced particularly strong fears, the capacity to focus inner attention may be severely harmed, for fear now works with increased intensity from its position within ego consciousness, effecting a nearly complete separation of ordinary consciousness from all other modes of consciousness.

How do fears find their way from the world to take up hidden residence within ego consciousness? Through the body, where fearful constrictions can reverberate into consciousness, and through fearful experiences retained as memories. Also, the culture we live in fosters these fearful reverberations—a culture that leaves no room for living connections with the spiritual realms. While connections with angels, spirit guides, or the dead are more openly discussed now, such experiences are still seen as part of a cultural fringe and are often met with skepticism. The enormous comfort and guidance that can come from such experiences provide an antidote to fear. If these kind of realities have no place in culture, fear finds its way into ego consciousness unimpeded.

Furthering Development of Ego Consciousness

Since the very structure of ego consciousness incorporates fear, broadening the range of consciousness is one way to work against the domination of fear. The process of deepening consciousness can be an everyday practice in which we work toward becoming more oriented toward soul life. The idea is not to bring soul life into ordinary consciousness but, rather, to bring ordinary consciousness into soul consciousness.

How might this be practiced? Rather than trying to give attention to the soul, we must try to be available for it to get our attention. Image, the soul's reality, is a capacity of the imagination—not inner pictures to be looked at, but the process of picturing, which is every moment forming and just as quickly dissolving. The content of an inner picture is but the outer clothing, a conclusive moment of the imaging process. Thus, we should not pay as much attention to the image content as to the feelings, the impressions, the sense of movement, rhythm, and the dramatic action of the picturing process.

Suppose I have a dream of flying without wings over a city. Suddenly, at the moment in the dream that I realize I am flying, I start to fall. A small brown dog, standing on the street where I am about to land, looks up, curious, but also with a look of recognition, as if it knows this falling body. At that moment, the fall stops, and I ascend again into the clouds. The dream image grabs my attention when I awaken. From the viewpoint of ego consciousness, perhaps the dream means that I am too much caught by the spirit, which makes me act as if I need no solid ground and can float around willy-nilly; but as soon as I can connect my spirit with the animal in me, then my spirit is free in a new way. A clever interpretation, but all nonsense! If, however, upon waking I work to hold the dream image as a whole, then I remain closer to the soul's own expression. Dreaming, as with all image activity, is not linear. Putting a dream into narrative form is itself already a form of interpretation. If I can feel and sense every layer of the dream simultaneously rather than as a narrative, I nourish, honor, and support the soul in its own mode of action.

Soul life does not conform to the ego's logic. When we attempt to understand the soul through ordinary logic rather than letting it instruct us in its own ways, we strengthen the forces of the ego and weaken those of soul life. However, the ego does not have to be abandoned in order for soul to have its say, and in fact doing so can only result in being overwhelmed by experiences that we will be unable to understand and hold. When the fear within ego consciousness is reduced, then the true nature of ego as the very spiritual center of our being functions freely. Rather than being opposed to wider and deeper forms of consciousness, the central "I" welcomes such experiences. To paraphrase the great poet Samuel Taylor Coleridge, the ego, free of fear, is the repetition within the finite mind of the infinite "I am."

The intention of gradually coming to sense the soul's own mode of activity is to allow ourselves to be changed by the soul. Dreams are an excellent place to begin because in them we can confront the rudimentary elements of a logic different from that exercised by ego consciousness. This new logic of simultaneity, if we immerse ourselves in it, begins to change cognition, memory, thinking, and perception in waking life. This alteration does not simply involve knowing ourselves more fully, but, more significant, it involves a change in the capacities through which we approach the world and others. The invisible hold that fears have on our consciousness loosens.

As the stronghold of fear within ego consciousness diminishes, we become able to find more soul qualities within the world. In waking life, the soul is the inner enjoyer of all that presents itself to us. To speak of the soul as the enjoyer does not mean to imply that it is interested only in gratification; soul enjoys everything, even things we might judge as reprehensible. To let the soul qualities of the world grab our attention requires that we become ever more conscious of the world as a process of images coming into being.

I spend a few moments every day consciously making an inner image of something that appeared to me in the world that day. I might, for example, have driven down the road from my house in the mountains after a snow-storm and seen the snow-covered trees lining the road, a very impressive and moving sight. This is not yet a con-scious soul experience if the event was observed and then the next event was allowed to take over. At night, I spend five minutes making an inner image of the scene I saw ear-lier in the day. I do not just remember what I saw, and I do not just visualize it with the inner eye. Visualization is like looking at an inner picture before one's eyes and is primarily a mental activity. Rather, what is required here is to make a very detailed, exact image, and then to let this image pervade my whole being so that it no longer appears as if in front of me, but, rather, I become the image. The work here is to stabilize the image so that it does not quickly fade or turn into something else.

This kind of exercise does not have to be confined to visual things. I practice such imaging with music, with a phrase someone has spoken, with touch, smells, the full range of our senses. The same sort of exercise applies not only to things perceived but also to thoughts, feelings, actions, the whole field of human experiences.

As the soul strengthens, imaginal ego consciousness develops. We do not have to obliterate ordinary consciousness to have soul experiences; rather, the aim is to bring imaginal consciousness into closer connection with ordinary consciousness. The world itself then begins to appear more as a constant activity than as fixed contents. Suppose I look out my window at the landscape every day. Because of the constant change of light and shadow, of clouds and sun, of mist and wind, objects change shape and group themselves in different ways at different times. A tree may at one moment be central, and at another moment be part of the background. Coloring may vary from blue to silver to shades of indigo and purple. The world-as-image is constantly coming into being in different ways, ever new.

All the world is available for soul-making. The constructed world, built by human ingenuity, presents itself as image activity. A sleek, glassy, towering skyscraper stands alone on a corner, fragile, isolated, and closed in on itself, and my heart goes out to this lonely building. Other human beings present themselves, too. What an amazement to observe, for example, how strongly a person walks, feet firmly planted, as if at the next moment the weight of a leg may be far too much to lift and he may be forever frozen in that spot. How, one wonders, is it possible that he moves at all? Another person seems to fly through the air, barely bothering to touch the ground with each step. Or to look at the countenance of a person's face——one face, lined, wrinkled, creviced, the sorrows, joys, woes of a lifetime made visible; another smooth, delicate skin, all her life experiences instead showing forth through deep, dark, pensive eyes.

Finding soul in the world is not an act of projection. This is a psychological invention, created by a sharp dividing line placed between ego consciousness and the rest of soul life, which relegates the latter to "the unconscious." From the viewpoint of this kind of psychology, soul qualities are not part of the world; they come from the unconscious and are projected into the world. Once the fear hidden within ego consciousness bubbles to the surface and is exposed, however, we can see clearly that it is fear that separates ego consciousness from other modes of soul life.

Working to bring soul into relation with ego consciousness not only leaves fear without a place to hide within us, but also has an effect on fear in the world. As soul life gradually becomes more conscious, we feel as if a part of ourselves passes over into whatever comes to us, whether from the depths within or the expanses without. Such feeling is not in the realm of out-of-body or mystical experiences. Rather, everything we call soul is but a variation, a modification of one sort or another of the creative activity of love. Love does overcome fear, but not the kind of love that we engage in from our ego or sentimentality. Love acts as a force against fear by being an impulse toward relationship, connection, and attraction, which stands against impulses toward separation, division, conflict, and violence. As we become more soul conscious, we find ourselves more and more in the world and less and less self-centered. Rather than wait for love to come to us, hoping to be swept up by this divine force, we are now called on to do our part to add to the circulation of love in the world as the primary antidote to the overwhelming amount of fear everywhere.

Fear and the Intellect

Fear's presence within ego consciousness has its most devastating effect in the domain of our thinking. When we use cognition, memory, and perception to develop the intellect, fear inserts itself into the process, soul life is cut off from ordinary consciousness, and thinking becomes unhealthy. This is not to say that the contents of what one thinks about are unhealthy, but that the act of thinking itself takes on a structure that works in collusion with fear.

While thinking can be a soul activity, for most of us it remains an act of ego consciousness. When I say that thinking can be a soul activity, I mean here cognition, the capacity to know through the forming of ideas. Ideas are images—the word *idea* comes from the Greek *eidos,* meaning "image." When fear enters deeply into consciousness, the capacity of forming ideas as images diminishes. We experience ideas almost completely in their utilitarian and functional dimension rather than in their sacred dimension.

Cognitive imagination works by weaving together the two polarities necessary for the forming of ideas, differentiation and wholeness. (Polarities are not opposites but exist in tandem, one needing the other, just as light cannot exist without the darkness.[3]) Ordinary thinking is dominated by the pole of differentiation. We divide, separate, analyze, scrutinize, take things apart, break them down into smaller and smaller pieces, rationalize. What we know in this way are abstractions, not the fullness of reality. This way of thinking loses sight of the whole and makes the world of concepts cold and devoid of a healthy feeling component. And yet so-called holistic thinking, which has arisen to counterbalance the damage done by centuries of the analytic mode, runs the risk of being unclear, fuzzy, overgeneralized, sentimentalized, lacking in particularity. Neither of these forms of thinking counts as imaginal cognition. What splits the two polarities is the covert presence of fear at the center of ordinary consciousness, fear that prompts cognition to mistrust imagination and imagination to distrust cognition.

Weighting thought on the side of differentiation flattens our cognitive life with abstractions. We come to see something in one dimension only, and make that single aspect into the whole. Fear grabs hold of this presentation of reality and uses it to turn thinking into argumentation. We defend our one-sided point of view, unable to take in the many sides of the question. We begin to imagine that the whole point of thinking is to come to a conclusion, which further damages the possibility of imaginal cognition. Once we are embedded in this notion, we no longer are thinking but are merely stringing together thoughts to reach a conclusion. Such thinking does nothing to bring creativity to the world. Our minds merely grasp after thoughts that are already completed and circulating in the world like old worn coins.

The interweaving of the polarities of differentiation and wholeness produces a kind of thinking that has warmth and subtlety and is essentially artistic in nature. An artist, for example, visualizes the whole painting he's working on and at the same time sees each discreet part of the painting in relation to the others. Although he doesn't try to picture the finished painting before he begins to paint, which would be like trying to transfer an abstraction to the canvas, the true artist has a quite clear sense of the whole and of how the particularities of the painting will bring this whole to light. The whole is utterly real but invisible; it becomes visible only through its constituent parts. Imaginal cognition has this quality. Just as a musician does not just string notes together but makes the whole song present throughout each of its parts, imaginal cognition is a kind of orchestration. We can work toward making our daily life an act of artistic cognition, paying attention to how everything we do relates to a whole context, consisting of our relations with others, with the world, and with the spiritual and soul realms.

Thinking in the mode of differentiation and analysis is more suitable for the material aspects of reality, while thinking in the mode of wholeness is more suited to spiritual aspects of reality. Unfortunately, these two domains tend to go their own directions, which is exactly what fear wants. Scientific thinking, for example, has developed the mode of differentiation to its highest degree, whereas religious thinking and spiritual thinking have developed wholeness. Both scientific and religious thought inspire a fantasy of hope, but neither does much to make hope an actual experience. Uniting these two into a new form of imaginal thinking can go a long way toward diminishing fear in the world, restoring hope to the act of cognition.

Thought as an Independent Reality

We are surrounded by and penetrated with spirit and soul realities. These realities are not to be thought of in the way we think of material realities. Spirits, angels, and the dead are continually with us. Their presence can be experienced, provided we first develop capacities of imaginal cognition. To think in this new way will begin to reveal more of reality than we have thus far dreamed of, but it does more than this. Thinking of any kind does not remain confined to our heads. Every thought we produce radiates into the world and exists as a magnet, attracting to it thoughts of a similar nature. If we just consider this possibility for a moment, what at first sounds utterly strange may begin to seem plausible.

How did the analytic mode of thinking spread itself throughout the world? This kind of thinking has not always characterized human thought, and at first it must have seemed very strange indeed. Did it spread in the world only through education? Education refined it, but education cannot account for its emergence or its adoption as a norm of thought. This type of thinking, although carried out individual by individual, exerts an independent force in the world, where certain thoughts, once freed from those who produce them, combine and gather strength. This is how this type of thinking begins to have real power. Analytic thinking has gradually pulled all of humanity into a current of will that is isolated and independent from the invisible realities that surround us.

When a person is in love, that love does not remain enclosed within the individual. It radiates and can be felt by others. We say, "You're beaming." Thought radiates in the same way. By working to engage in imaginal cognition, we radiate new kinds of thinking into the world and build a new current of collective thought—cognition that is an interweaving of differentiation and wholeness, thinking that is not dry and abstract but warm and nuanced. What is new about this current of thought is that it attracts not only the thoughts of other human beings but also the currents of the invisible worlds—the worlds of the gods, the spirits, the angels, the dead. The horizontal world of everyday life can then intermingle with the vertical world of the eternal. We experience these currents from the spiritual realms as moments of inspiration.

We cannot diminish fear in the world on our own. All of the exercises presented here are oriented to becoming open and available to spiritual currents working through the soul, and it is only with the assistance of these currents that fear can be diminished. This sense of inspiration needs to be distinguished from religious thought. Although religion has a certain affinity with such currents, and attracts them, I am not suggesting that if we give ourselves over to religion it will take care of fear in the world.

Inspiration, as described here, is a capacity of feeling-knowing. Say, for example, you are pondering. Your thought becomes a strong magnet within you, pulling ideas, sentiments, currents of feeling together. Similarly, imaginal cognition is a magnet that attracts spiritual presences. When we enact this kind of living thinking—thinking within the reality of things themselves, which creates rather than simply uses ideas—it forms a bridge to the invisible worlds that are all around us. Inspiration of this type has nothing in common with channeling, mediums, or psychic powers that bring messages from the spirit realms. The feeling-knowing of imaginal cognition can become part of our everyday, waking awareness. Bringing it to fruition is our task.

To be able to feel the current of inspiration, it is necessary to loosen the hold that fears have on the body. The body, caught in anxiety, is too constricted to feel the current of inspiration. To be able to feel this current, it is also necessary to have worked at developing imaginal consciousness, for inspiration will have to be experienced by the soul. It cannot be felt by ordinary ego consciousness. Intellect caught in the separation of the polarities of differentiation and wholeness also cannot feel this current of inspiration. Thus, working toward healing the body, the soul, and thinking is necessary for inspiration to flower.

Inspiration does not come to us fully realized. We do not usually receive full-blown ideas, complete and ready to be implemented. Inspiration has a quality analogous to touch, and although we feel it in the cognitive domain, it nevertheless reverberates subtly in the body. Everyone has experienced moments of inspiration in life, but the point is to develop such moments into an ongoing reality. For example, you may feel as if someone you have known who has died is present to you. You do not see that person, but feel a presence like a light touch. These kinds of experiences can be strengthened, for although we are usually not aware enough to catch hold of such fleeting feelings, they are going on all the time. Such feelings have more significance than a momentary brush with the invisible worlds. If we take them seriously, cognition begins to change. We not only begin to let more spiritual things enter our thought, but the structure of our thinking itself also begins to change, becoming more open, more flexible, less materialistic, more receptive and dynamic.

What happens to the fear that has lived for so long within the structure of our ego consciousness as cognition expands? As one becomes accustomed to the touch of inspiration, something very interesting happens to the fear hidden within ego consciousness. It does not simply go away but drops into the fertile womb of the soul, where it undergoes a transformation. This process typically takes the following form. At first we feel a kind of exhaustion. This exhaustion is not so much physical—it may feel a little bit like depression, but it does not have quite the same heaviness. It is more like a feeling of releasing something very heavy that's been held for a long time. The exhaustion thus carries with it a sense of relief. We feel the fatigue of the soul that has so long been suppressed.

We see this feeling of fatigue on the face of practically everyone, though it is not usually accompanied by a sense of relief. We recognize inwardly that the structure within which the world has operated for so many years cannot be sustained much longer. This structure consists of a vast economic, technocratic, and political order that emphasizes individualism, consumerism, self-centeredness, and political and corporate power. Within this order, human beings are challenged to find individual meaning and purpose. We seek them in family values, religion, and education, but these tend to be oriented toward serving the status quo rather than fostering self-knowledge.

Along with the deep feeling of exhaustion and release, however, a yearning appears. It is felt as a yearning to create out of an entirely new center rather than out of intellectual consciousness, a yearning to think from the center of the heart, through the capacity of love. While thinking is not abandoned for feeling, the search for feeling-thinking can begin in earnest. The norm of this new thinking will be to think logically as well as beautifully and artistically.

The Necessity of Developing Powers of Attention

The suggestions given in this chapter rely on developing the ability to concentrate, to freely give our attention to matters that do not ordinarily occupy us. When waking from a dream, for example, we can allow the dream to instruct us concerning its own mode of activity by holding it as a whole image rather than seeking to dissect its meaning. To be able to hold an image in this way requires attentiveness; it requires that we direct our interest to one single object to the exclusion of all else for a period of time. Or to be able to observe something—the inner image of a rose, say—to the point where the most subtle qualities of the image become apparent demands that other ideas or images are not, during the period of concentration, allowed to enter.

All of the exercises thus far described require that, for a time, we shut out everything else, all cares and worries, all extraneous thinking. Doing these concentration exercises leads gradually to the development of imaginal cognition. When we came to the discussion of imaginal cognition, no special exercises were offered, because the way we arrive at this new form of knowing is indirect, by developing the soul qualities in our consciousness. In this reflection on fear and consciousness, however, it is necessary to say something about attention itself.

What role does attention play in consciousness? Attention is an act of volition, of the will, of being present to something like a radiance of light. Some attention is necessary to be conscious of anything, but attention itself is pre-cognitive. It is a power behind consciousness, making consciousness possible. I can turn my attention to something, and while it is possible to be aware of attention, we cannot be fully conscious of our attention itself.

All the exercises thus far described are not concerned primarily with the content of the images given. Rather, they concern strengthening the power of attention. Through practicing these exercises, the pre-cognitive quality of attention actually becomes conscious, what has been referred to as a witness consciousness.[4]

The forces of attention need development because in our time we do not give our attention freely, out of soul forces, but find our attention captured. Something is always taking our attention—television, computers, entertainment, movies, work, the needs and demands of others. We are rapidly becoming more and more passive in our awareness. Even the practice of meditation has produced an array of technical devices, items ranging from guided meditation tapes to special goggles with flashing lights supposedly timed to induce meditative states. Meditating requires maintaining a constant, continuous state of full attention, an extremely active consciousness.

The phenomenon of attention tells us something most important about the reality of the soul. Although we do not create our own soul, its presence will go unnoticed without our attention. Without attention, soul disperses. Soul exercises aim to build up the strength of attention so that it gradually becomes continuous. If we do not take up this work of attention ourselves, we cannot approach the world with a fresh creativity, because our soul consciousness is trapped by preconceived forms coming at us externally. These forms are received by the soul, but if the soul itself does not apply attention to what it creates, it will remain shrouded in fear. The soul's fear in this case is of its own demise and actually constitutes the deepest of all fears. This fear is nothing other than existential dread.

While attention constitutes a very active state, its activity consists of pure receptivity. If I give full attention to an inner image, and then focus on the attention itself, what presents itself? Pure stillness, which is like an eternal beam of light. We could say that attention essentially consists in performing the act of inner stillness. Why not then practice stillness directly rather than trying to achieve such a state by focusing on some inner content? Because stillness alone would result in the state of sleep. Stillness in the presence of some object of attention does not put us to sleep but rather enhances consciousness, putting us in a waking state that otherwise resembles sleep.

Another important reason for concentrating on images rather than seeking pure emptiness lies in the fact that conscious attention makes us actively receptive to soul and spirit realities. These archetypal presences, while not belonging to the sense world, nonetheless belong to the realm of light, sound, color, and scent. The earthly world and the soul and spirit worlds form one world. The "beyond" is all around us, and our link to it is maintained through subtle states that resemble sense qualities. The sense-like qualities of soul and spirit are much more mobile and dynamic than the sense qualities of material objects, so the way to them consists of giving attention to the subtle qualities of inner images.

When one takes up practices such as meditation, active imagination, visualization, or the kinds of concentration suggested here, an expectation arises that something spectacular or at least mildly spectacular will occur. When, after a while, nothing of this nature occurs, the initial excitement of developing other modes of consciousness decreases, and one may decide not to continue the practices. The object of the exercises, however, is to perform them regularly.

The most significant moments for the development of other modes of consciousness are the moments after completing the concentration. During these moments, the effects of the state we have engaged in work on us; it is therefore important after every exercise to remain calm, to not leave the state of concentration and enter into normal activity. Once an intensity of concentration has been developed by doing the exercises quite regularly, we will feel an inner calm, a sense of being graced, a vitality in the body, and an open space of inner freedom.

Concentration works on us in this way, and gradually more of these qualities enter ongoing daily life.

These exercises also develop a sense of gratitude, even when no spectacular results follow. Feeling gratitude after each practice increases the ability to continue such practices, for gratitude makes a vessel of the soul, increasing its receptivity.

When we expect dramatic results from concentrating on inner images, we are being led by the habit of utilitarian value, which harbors the specter of fear. The fear within utilitarian value operates by urging us to move as quickly as possible from our acts of concentration to doing something, producing something, demonstrating our self-worth. The fear, however, always hides itself, and we see only what appears to be achievement. Waging war, for example, seems to have the utilitarian value of producing peace, but the individuals killed in the process are reported as mere statistics. Or electronic technologies produce the utilitarian value of speed of communication, but we are not aware of the fear that arises from living at a speed that bears no relation to the rhythms of the body. The values brought into the world through concentrated acts of attention devoted to the soul life lie in the realms of love, art, and beauty, which, from a utilitarian point of view, do not seem to do anything. These values balance the life activities that have stepped beyond their bounds and are bringing fear into the world. If we apply utilitarian values to our inner work, then concentration will merely bring more fear into the world.

No one can deny the tremendous power and influence the intellect has in the world. Primarily through the development of the rational, differentiating intellect, we have come to know the world in its material dimensions and have developed the technologies to control it for our own purposes. The spiritual worlds have been placed completely outside the everyday world, in the beyond. But we mustn't forget that there is no division between this world and the beyond. Fear wishes to keep this revelation from us, for if we realize this truth the power of fear is diminished. We invent the idea of a division because we are not able to see everything, and what we cannot perceive we relegate to the great beyond. The beyond is all we cannot perceive with ordinary consciousness, but simply because something cannot be perceived does not mean that it is not present right here, all around us.

Notes

INTRODUCTION

1. Rudolf Steiner, *Psychoanalysis and Spiritual Psychology*, introduction by Robert Sardello (Hudson, NY: Anthroposophic Press, 1990).
2. Rudolf Steiner, *A Psychology of Body, Soul, and Spirit*, introduction by Robert Sardello (Hudson, NY: Anthroposophic Press, 1999).

CHAPTER 1

1. Rather than derive my definition of soul from the psychology of C. G. Jung, which takes soul to be a factor completely autonomous from any influence from the immediate surrounding world, I propose a broader view based on the understanding of soul provided by Rudolf Steiner. In particular, see his *A Psychology of Body, Soul, and Spirit*, introduction by Robert Sardello (Hudson, NY: Anthroposophic Press, 1999).
2. I am grateful to Sabine Cox for this description, written as

part of a correspondence course on fear offered by the School of Spiritual Psychology.

3. Rudolf Steiner's criticism of Jung's understanding of the soul was that it did not go far enough. When Jung describes the archetypal figures of soul life, he never understands these figures as being outside of the psyche. Steiner's view is that psychic life is affected by invisible but quite real imaginal realities that are not part of individual psychic life itself. The view of fear taken in this book imagines it as this kind of presence.

4. A further view of the soul is implied here. Soul does not exist within us but only in and through our relationships with others and with the world. This view follows yet another approach to psychology, the approach of phenomenological psychology. See, for example, J. H. Van den Berg, *A Different Existence* (Pittsburgh: Duquesne University Press, 1971).

5. Rudolf Steiner, *Love and Its Meaning in the World* (Hudson, NY: Anthroposophic Press, 1999).

6. For the background and development of this method, see Dennis Klocek, *Seeking Spirit Vision* (Fair Oaks, CA: Rudolf Steiner College Press, 1998).

CHAPTER 2

1. The understanding of the body as an intimate engagement with the world is central to phenomenological psychology, which is based on a non-dualistic view of body and world. See Maurice Merleau-Ponty, *The Phenomenology of Perception* (London: Routledge, 1992).

2. I am well aware that the changes in the body mentioned are the result of increased flow of adrenaline. Recognizing the route through which organs are affected, however, does not change the fact that very subtle wounds of the organs occur as a result of fear.

3. Rudolf Steiner, *Anthroposophy (A Fragment)* (Hudson, NY: Anthroposophic Press, 1996). See also Robert Sardello and Cheryl Sanders, "Care of the Senses: A Neglected Dimension of Education," in Jeffery Kane, ed., *Education, Information, and Imagination: Essays on Learning and Thinking* (Columbus, OH: PrenticeHall/Merril, 1999).

4. The Virtual Alchemy Web Page, www.levity.com, operated by Adam McLean.

CHAPTER 3

1. Charles B. Strozier, *Apocalypse: On the Psychology of Fundamentalism in America* (Boston: Beacon Press, 1994).

2. Bernard Lievegoed, *Man on the Threshold* (Stroud, England: Hawthorn Press, 1985).

3. For a phenomenological description of duration and tempo, see J. H. Van den Berg, *Things* (Pittsburgh: Duquesne University Press, 1973).

4. Ron Dunselman, *In Place of the Self: How Drugs Work* (Stroud, England: Hawthorn Press, 1995).

5. I am grateful to Charles Blum for these descriptions.

6. For a series of meditations of this type, see Georg Kuhlewind, *From Normal to Healthy: Paths to the Liberation of Consciousness* (Hudson, NY: Lindisfarne Press, 1988).

7. These descriptions were written by students in a workshop entitled "Freeing the Soul from Fear," offered by the School of Spiritual Psychology.

8. *The Zen Teachings of Bodhidharma,* trans. Red Pine (New York: North Point Press, 1997), p. 47.

CHAPTER 4

1. Betty S. Flowers, *The Economic Myth* (Austin: Center for Communications, University of Texas, 1993).

2. The person who wrote this description asked not to be identified.

3. Baruch Urieli, "Man's Approach to the Spirit Today and the Sacrifice of Caspar Hauser," *Camphill Correspondence*, August 1984, pp. 1–6.

4. See, for example, Thomas Moore, *The Planets Within* (Lewisburg, PA: Bucknell University Press, 1982).

5. See, for example, Rudolf Steiner, *The Riddle of Humanity* (London: Rudolf Steiner Press, 1990).

6. See, for example, Victor Bott, *Anthroposophical Medicine* (New York: Thorsons, 1984).

CHAPTER 5

1. See Walter Enloe and Randy Morris, *Encounters with Hiroshima* (St. Paul, MN: Hamline University Press, 1998), and Michael Perlman, *Hiroshima Forever: The Ecology of Mourning* (Barrytown, NY: Station Hill Arts, 1995).

2. James Hillman, *Pan and the Nightmare* (Dallas: Spring Publications, 1965).

3. Theodore Roszak, Mary E. Gomes, and Allen D. Kanner, eds., *Ecopsychology: Restoring the Earth, Healing the Mind* (San Francisco: Sierra Club Books, 1995).

4. Rudolf Steiner, *The Spiritual Hierarchies and the Physical World* (Hudson, NY: Anthroposophic Press, 1996).

5. See Rudolf Steiner, *Anthroposophy (A Fragment)* (Hudson, NY: Anthroposophic Press, 1996), pp. 106–120.

6. This exercise is adapted from Dennis Klocek, *Seeking Spirit Vision* (Fair Oaks, CA: Rudolf Steiner College Press, 1998).

7. This view of obsession is from Arthur Guirdham, *Obsession* (Essex, England: C. W. Daniel, 1971).

8. Kevin T. Dann, *Bright Colors Falsely Seen: Synaesthesia and the*

Search for Transcendental Knowledge (New Haven: Yale University Press, 1998).

9. James Hillman and Marie-Louise Von Franz, *Lectures on Jung's Typology: The Inferior Function and the Feeling Function* (Dallas: Spring Publications, 1971).

CHAPTER 6

1. Otto Rank, *The Double: A Psychoanalytic Study* (Chapel Hill: University of North Carolina Press, 1971).

2. Guy de Maupassant, "The Horla," in *Pierre and Jean and Selected Short Stories,* trans. Lowell Bair (New York: Bantam, 1969), pp. 286–297.

3. Robert Jay Lifton, *The Nazi Doctors: Medical Killing and the Psychology of Genocide* (New York: Basic Books, 1986).

4. Novalis, *Henry von Ofterdingen* (New York: Frederick Ungar, 1964).

CHAPTER 7

1. Rudolf Steiner, *Love and Its Meaning in the World* (Hudson, NY: Anthroposophic Press, 1998).

2. Rainer Maria Rilke, *Rilke on Love and Other Difficulties,* trans. John J. L. Mood (New York: W. W. Norton, 1993), pp. 33–34.

3. Novalis, *Pollen and Fragments,* trans. Arthur Versluis (Port Huron, MI: Phanes Press, 1989), p. 62.

4. Ibid., p. 118.

5. Ibid., p. 59.

6. Rilke, *Rilke on Love,* p. 27.

7. Novalis, *Pollen,* p. 41.

CHAPTER 8

1. Michael Howard, ed., *Art as Spiritual Activity: Rudolf Steiner's Contribution to the Visual Arts* (Hudson, NY: Anthroposophic Press, 1998).

2. Ibid., pp. 135–154.

3. I am grateful to Louise Cowan, professor of literature at the University of Dallas, for introducing me to this comprehensive view of the literary imagination.

4. Howard, *Art as Spiritual Activity,* pp. 176–194.

5. Ibid., pp. 272–281.

CHAPTER 9

1. Georg Kuhlewind, *Stages of Consciousness: Meditations on the Boundaries of the Soul* (West Stockbridge, MA: Inner Traditions/Lindisfarne Press, 1984).

2. Georg Kuhlewind, *From Normal to Healthy: Paths to the Liberation of Consciousness* (Hudson, NY: Lindisfarne Press, 1988).

3. Dennis Klocek, *Seeking Spirit Vision* (Fair Oaks, CA: Rudolf Steiner College Press, 1998), pp. 11–21.

4. Georg Kuhlewind, *The Life of the Soul* (Hudson, NY: Lindisfarne Press, 1990).

Acknowledgments

I thank Katie Boyle, my agent, for her constant encouragement and sensitive guidance during the time it took to get this book from initial manuscript to final form. The Ann and Erlo Van Waveren Foundation provided funding to help me with the basic writing. Cheryl Sanders supported the writing with untiring conversation and depth of heart. I am grateful to Amy Hertz for doing truly masterly and artistic editing, cutting out endless wandering bypaths to come to the core. After radical surgery was done on the text, Chris Knutsen gave much of his heart forces to bring this book back to life. I cannot thank him enough for his careful and exquisite work. I thank all the students of the School of Spiritual Psychology in every part of the country for their insightful contributions to the ideas. Therese Schroeder-Sheker of the Chalice of Repose Project unceasingly supported the soul level of this work. Gail Thomas and Larry Allums of the Dallas Institute of Humanities and Culture encouraged the presentations of these ideas in ongoing seminars and conversations. Christopher Bamford, a true soul friend, kept me intellectually honest. I also express my gratitude to Carol Hegedus and Rob Lehman of the John E. Fetzer Institute for believing that the work of the School of Spiritual Psychology can help reduce fear in the world.

Research for the book was conducted as part of the work of the School of Spiritual Psychology. Individuals named in this book gave permission for the use of their workshop descriptions. This school offers courses, seminars, conferences, soul retreats, and consulting on the development of soul capacities. The activities of the school are offered in various parts of the country. Information can be obtained by writing to:

School of Spiritual Psychology
PO Box 5099
Greensboro, North Carolina 27435